BANKING ON WORDS

BANKING ON WORDS

THE FAILURE OF LANGUAGE IN
THE AGE OF DERIVATIVE FINANCE

Arjun Appadurai

The University of Chicago Press

Chicago & London

Arjun Appadurai is the Goddard Professor of Media, Culture, and Communication at New York University and a senior fellow of the Institute for Public Knowledge. A fellow of the American Academy of Arts and Sciences, he is the author or editor of numerous books, including *The Social Life of Things*, *Modernity at Large, Fear of Small Numbers*, and *The Future as Cultural Fact*.

The University of Chicago Press, Chicago 60637
The University of Chicago Press, Ltd., London
© 2016 by The University of Chicago
All rights reserved. Published 2016.
Printed in the United States of America

25 24 23 22 21 20 19 18 17 16   1 2 3 4 5

ISBN-13: 978-0-226-31863-9 (cloth)
ISBN-13: 978-0-226-31877-6 (paper)
ISBN-13: 978-0-226-31880-6 (e-book)
DOI: 10.7208/chicago/9780226318806.001.0001

Library of Congress Cataloging-in-Publication Data
Appadurai, Arjun, 1949– author.
Banking on words : the failure of language in the age of derivative finance / Arjun Appadurai.
pages cm
Includes bibliographical references and index.
ISBN 978-0-226-31863-9 (cloth : alk. paper) — ISBN 978-0-226-31877-6 (pbk. : alk. aper) — ISBN
978-0-226-31880-6 (e-book) 1. Derivative securities—Social aspects. 2. Global Financial Crisis,
2008–2009. I. Title.
HG6024.A3A67 2015
332.64'57014—dc23
2015009033

♾ This paper meets the requirements of ANSI/NISO Z39.48–1992 (Permanence of Paper).

CONTENTS

PREFACE

This book has its roots in the early 1970s, when I was a graduate student at the Committee on Social Thought at the University of Chicago. I was exposed then to the writings of Max Weber (though I first read *The Protestant Ethic and the Spirit of Capitalism* in 1967, as an undergraduate at Brandeis University). During the five decades that have elapsed since then, Max Weber has been both my inspiration and my foil. This book is an effort to offer Weber, on whose shoulders I (and many others) still rest, a small gift in return. It is also a tribute to my graduate education at the University of Chicago at a time when anthropology and the other social sciences hosted a uniquely fruitful conversation about the future of what were then called "the new nations." Anthropology and economics have had less to say to each other since then. I hope this book will add to the arguments in favor of deepening their dialogue.

I have had the pleasure of developing many of the ideas in this book in close and intense conversations with the members of the Cultures of Finance group at New York University: Randy Martin, Robert Meister, Ben Lee, Edward LiPuma, Robert Wosnitzer, and, more recently, Emanuel Derman and Elie Ayache. I have also benefited from opportunities to present some of this work at WISER (The Wits Institute for Social and Economic Research) in Johannesburg; the Human Economy project at the University of Pretoria; the Anthropology Departments at New York University and the University of Cambridge; the University of Copenhagen; and the Institute for Public Knowledge at New York University.

The numerous conferences, workshops, and seminars of the Cultures of Finance group were made possible by the financial generosity of the provost of NYU, and the successive directors of the Institute for Public Knowledge, Craig Calhoun and Eric Klinenberg. During these occasions I was the beneficiary of the work of some of the best scholars (including many younger ones) working on social science approaches to finance in the New York area, elsewhere in the United States, and in other countries. Randy Martin's book, *Knowledge LTD: Toward a Social Logic of the Derivative* (2015), a collected volume of papers by members of the Cultures of Finance group (currently being prepared for publication), and the recent doctoral dissertation of Robert Wosnitzer, all reflect lines of thought from this collective dialogue, which is a major context for this book. I have also benefited greatly from the encouragement and intellectual conviviality of my colleagues and students in the Department of Media, Culture, and Communication at the Steinhardt School, New York University.

I owe special thanks to Keith Hart, Ben Lee, and Natasha Schull, who read the entire manuscript and made several valuable suggestions which I have done my best to address in this book. I owe sincere thanks as well to Madhurim Gupta, who helped with every detail of the preparation of this manuscript for publication.

In addition to my colleagues in the Cultures of Finance group at NYU, I have received scholarly support, encouragement, and fruitful criticism about the ideas in this book from the following friends and colleagues: Ritu Birla, Craig Calhoun, Jean Comaroff, John Comaroff, Jane Guyer, Eric Klinenberg, Achille Mbembe, Uday Mehta, Stine Puri, Vyjayanthi Rao, Hylton White, and Caitlin Zaloom.

My wife, Gabika Bockaj, has made our years together an ongoing reminder of the pleasures and passions of a true partnership. Its living gift is our son, Kabir, who has done his joyous best to make my waking hours more disciplined than ever. This book is for them.

Arjun Appadurai
New York City
January 2015

CHAPTER ONE

THE LOGIC OF PROMISSORY FINANCE

The Argument in Brief

The principal argument of this book is that the failure of the financial system in 2007–8 in the United States was primarily a failure of language. This argument does not deny that greed, ignorance, weak regulation, and irresponsible risk-taking were important factors in the collapse. But the new role of language in the marketplace is the condition of possibility for all these more easily identifiable flaws.

To make this case requires understanding how language takes on a new life in contemporary finance, and this argument takes us into a realm not usually explored when financial markets are discussed.[1] To understand how language takes on the role it does in finance today, four steps are involved. The first is to show how derivatives are the core technical innovation that characterizes contemporary finance. Edward LiPuma and Benjamin Lee took an initial step in this direction in their important book on *Financial Derivatives and the Globalization of Risk* (LiPuma and Lee 2004). Since then, there have been several efforts to define and explain derivatives, both within and outside the community of finance experts. The second step is to show how derivatives are, essentially, written contracts about the future prices of various types of financial assets, the essence of which are promises by the losing party to pay the winning party an agreed-upon sum of money in the event of a specific future price outcome. Thus the contract is a promise, and to understand it fully requires a new look at contracts, seen as promises about the uncertain future. This requires a re-examination of Marcel Mauss's classic study of *The Gift* (1990) and a rereading of J. L. Austin's work (1962) on performatives and their conditions of felicity. This analysis of derivative contracts brings out the special importance of language in the financial marketplace. A third step is to show how the derivative form exploits the linguistic power of the contract through the special form that money takes in the financial world, given that money is by definition the most abstract form in which the value of commodities can be expressed. A fourth and final step is to understand that the failure of the derivatives market (especially in the domain of housing mortgages) is primarily about *failed promises* (promises being the most important in Austin's typology of performatives), a type of failure that was neither occasional nor ad hoc but became systematic and contagious, thus bringing the entire financial market to the brink of disaster.

This introductory chapter elaborates this argument schematically and sequentially. The subsequent chapters look more closely at ideas about risk, ritual, salvation, performative failure, and (in)dividuality, by strategic rereadings of Emile Durkheim, Marcel Mauss, and Max Weber, to specify the links in this chain more carefully and more contextually. The last three chapters, about the politics of a different approach to derivatives and dividuals, point to a way of learning a progressive political lesson from the linguistic heart of contemporary finance.

The Derivative Form

Our current era of financialization is without precedent in the speed and scope of the innovations that have characterized it. Financialization may be broadly defined as the process that permits money to be used to make more money through the use of instruments that exploit the role of money in credit, speculation, and investment. Its deep historical roots lie in the epoch of the expansion of maritime trade and the growth of the idea of insurance against hazard for those merchants who shipped their trade goods across large oceanic distances during this period. Though this early period was still preoccupied by the divine and natural hazards that beset maritime commerce, the emergence of actuarial thinking in this time was the first effort to bring secular control to the likelihood of disaster at sea, and insurers began to offer means of protection to merchants who feared the loss of their goods at sea. The reasoning behind this early actuarial history was a mixture of theological and statistical perceptions of risk, and constitutes the first effort to distinguish statistically calculable risk from divine and natural uncertainty, a distinction that is the very foundation of modern finance.

The next big shift that is critical to the current power of finance is to be found in the commodity markets, notably in Chicago, in which traders first began to traffic in what became "futures," first of all in agrarian commodities (such as wheat and pork bellies) and gradually expanded to "futures" trades in all commodities with any significant market and unpredictable fluctuations in prices. Terms such as "put" and "call," "option" and "hedge," can be dated to these futures markets of the mid-nineteenth century, which remain important today, though to a smaller degree than in the period of their birth. In these futures markets, there was the first move toward separating the market in future prices from the market in current prices for commodities. These commodity futures are the earliest form of financial "assets" that are now distinguishable from the actual commodities whose prices underlay them. Today's derivatives (this term referring to the fact that future commodities are derivable from current commodities) are an extraordinary extension of these early futures contracts.

The link between the early history of insurance and the early history of futures market is that any risk of a positive change in prices (what we today call upside risks), about which a trader has doubts, can be offset, or in effect can be insured again, by taking a "hedge" position that protects traders who are convinced of a downside risk for the particular commodity price *in a specific time horizon*. The hedge is essentially a dynamic form of insurance.

What the derivative *is* and what it *does* are closely tied. The derivative is an asset whose value is based on that of another asset, which could itself be a derivative. In a chain of links that contemporary finance has made indefinitely long, the derivative is above all a linguistic phenomenon, since it is primarily a referent to something more tangible than itself: it is a proposition or a belief about another object that might itself be similarly derived from yet another similar object. Since the references and associations that compose a derivative chain have no status other than the credibility of their reference to something more tangible than themselves, the derivative's claim to value is essentially linguistic. Furthermore, its force is primarily performative, and is tied up with context, convention, and felicity. More specifically still, while the derivative is thus a linguistic artifact, it is even more specific in that it is an invitation to a performative insofar as a derivative takes full force when it is *traded*, that is, when two traders arrive at a written contract to exchange (buy and sell) a specific bundle of derivatives. The *promise* is for one of them to pay money to the other depending on who proves to be right about the future price (after a particular and specified temporal term) of that specific derivative. In this sense, of course, all contracts have a promissory element (Fried 1981). But the derivative form is the *sole* contractual form that is based on the unknown future value of an asset traded between two persons. Other contracts have known future values, known terms, and known current values (such as with loans, rents, and other pecuniary contracts). Thus, when an entire market driven by derivatives comes to the edge of collapse, there must be a deep underlying flaw in the linguistic world that derivatives presuppose.

The derivative form also poses a challenge to several different traditions of social science. Max Weber, who is engaged throughout this book, was a keen student of capitalism of his time, which covered the last decades of the nineteenth century and the first two decades of the twentieth century. He had a lifetime concern with defining, and then explaining, the rise of a peculiar form of capitalism in Europe in the eighteenth and nineteenth centuries. His most famous effort to account for this phenomenon was in his classic essay on *The Protestant Ethic and the Spirit of Capitalism* (2009). He stressed the uncertainty of salvation under the Calvinist dispensation but his account of the early capitalist merchants of Europe, essentially the first capitalist entrepreneurs, had no place for economic risk-taking, the latter being the very defining characteristic of the financialized capitalism of our times. This puzzle, and the lessons we can learn from Weber's apparent oversight, is the subject of several of the chapters to come, in which I argue that Weber's method and many of his key concepts help us to unpack the logic of contemporary finance.

Marx is a trickier case since he did the most to understand the special dynamics of industrial capitalism, and in his magnum opus, *Capital* (1992), he provided a new theory of production-based class formation, of the expropriation of value produced by the laboring classes of industrial capitalism, of the distinct place of surplus value in the creation of a new form of profit under industrial capitalism, of the production of commodity fetishism through the new role of money in mediating the life of the commodity form, and of the forms of power, consciousness, and hegemony produced by this transnational economic form. Yet, while Marx had a deep interest in the capitalist mode of investment and of the mysterious ways in which money reproduces itself, he did not give us any easy way to understand a form of capitalism that was barely born when he lived, that is, that sort of financialized capitalism in which the production of money by means of money (rather than of commodities by means of commodities) is the regnant form. For this reason, I do not engage Marx extensively in this book, though many of the thinkers with whom I do engage, notably Max Weber, had Marx as their primarily interlocutor.[2]

The initial insight that Weber offers us into the form of the derivative is that the root of the Calvinist ethic is radical uncertainty about salvation, or more precisely, radical uncertainty about the value of a person's life (as a whole) as a sign of his being one of the saved, thus one of the elect. Out of this soteriological dilemma grows, in Weber's view, a life dedicated to rational and methodical capitalist behavior, the goal of which is not profit for itself but profit as a sign of election. Since such a state of certainty about one's own election requires both speculation and certainty, it leads to a continuous wagering of oneself in the routines of methodical moneymaking. This curious transformation of salvational uncertainty into capitalist methodicality—the core of Weber's insight—offers a path into the radical risk-taking of the contemporary derivatives trader, whose interest in money becomes sufficiently obsessive as to make characterizations of his type through features like greed and outsize ego seem far too weak. This is the beginning of a way in which Weber, without quite seeing the coming autonomy of money as a means of making money through the derivative form, offers us a road into the ethos of derivative trading. This is the journey of some of the forthcoming chapters.

The Derivative Promise

The link between derivatives and language turns on the question of promises, which I view, following Austin, as one of the class of performatives, linguistic utterances that, if produced in the right conditions, create the conditions of their own truth. Elie Ayache, a derivatives trader and a French social thinker, has established the importance of seeing derivatives as written contracts. I engage his remarkable ideas primarily in chapter 6 of this book. I am indebted to him for establishing that derivatives, in the end, break free of the prison house of probability and that specific derivative trades, in real-time conditions, are best seen as written contracts. These contracts continuously create their own conditions of effectivity in a volatile market of future prices in which probability is at best a partial guide to what the two contracting parties agree upon when a derivative is sold and bought.

Ayache underlines the fact that the derivative trade is a time-bound contract about a definite future date on which an indefinite (or unpredictable) price might be set by the (future) market for a current derivative asset. He does not ponder the contractual side of the derivatives contract except to note that it is written, and therefore needs to be grasped as a written text about the unknown future, which commits the two trading parties to a specific transfer of money at a future date.

The idea that derivative trades are written contracts reminds us that Marcel Mauss's great essay on *The Gift* (1990) was a byproduct of his joint project with his colleague George Davy on the historical origins of the modern contract. Mauss wanted to understand what gave the contract its special force of compliance, outside of the strictures of coercion. He found the answer in the gift forms of ancient and primitive societies, and in the force of the *hau*, the spirit inherent in the gift that compels its return. In our current world, we might wish to ask where to locate the *hau* of the derivative. Chapters 3, 4, and 5 of this book are efforts to connect the modern derivative and the ancient gift, as forms of contract.

Mauss's effort to locate the *hau* of the gift, the force that compels its return in the spirit of reciprocity, was not entirely successful, because he did not fully see the vital role of language in gift forms, and the idea of the performative was not available to him. But his intuition that there was something in the ritualized process of gift and counter-gift that preceded the role of writing in contracts was brilliant. Though today's derivative contracts, like all modern contracts, are ideally in written form, their underlying force comes from the fact that they are composed of a mutual pair of promises, a promise to pay in one direction or another, at the expiry of a fixed period of time, and depending on the price of the derivative at that future time. This mutually binding promise is initially oral, and only incidentally committed to writing as confirmation and for the purposes of tracking and recordkeeping. A derivative trade is complete when the two traders, often on the phone, say, "It's done" (Wosnitzer 2014). This is a classic Austinian performative moment and it is the key to the *hau* of the derivative.

In Austinian terms, the conditions of felicity for this pair of promises to take its force include the mutual knowledge of the traders, the capacity of their larger institutions to fulfill the downside risk of large payments, and the general social network of managers, regulators, small shareholders, and large investors that lends an appropriate audience (even if virtual) for the transaction.

The systemic weakness of the larger financial system within which derivatives circulate is that it allows for the repeated commoditization of prior promises by new promises, thus diluting and disseminating the force of the promise across many players (traders) who bear only tiny portions of the burden of the larger interlinked system of promises that comprises the overall value of any particular derivatives market. This opens the systemic possibility of failure, breakdown, and collapse even when the bulk of individual trades meet their local conditions of felicity. This systemic dissemination of promises is connected to the idea of a performative chain, also discussed later in this chapter.[3] Put another way, when the contractual nature of the promise is subject to infinite further monetization, risks can be taken on prior risks and money can be made of speculative instruments that involve growing distances between derivatives and their underlying assets, which are frequently themselves derivative. This recursive chain of derivatives is the essence of the world of the subprime housing mortgage, explored further in chapter 4.

It is through the lens of housing mortgages that we can examine closely the sense in which the failure of the housing market that led up to the collapse of 2007–8, at its heart, was a linguistic failure. This argument interprets the indefinite dispersal and dissemination of promises, as well as the monetization of the entire series of promises, as opening the door to a massive disconnect between the ideal and the reality of the system of derivative trading.

Put simply, every derivative trade involves a winner and a loser, the one who pays at the end of the stipulated term, the new price, and the one who receives a payment. In principle this should create a perfect balance between winners and losers with no gains at the end of any given period across the entire system. Why does it not end up this way?

There are several reasons for this failure at a systemic level, in spite of a largely legal and rigorous system of reciprocal promises at the level of the individual contract. The housing market offers a clear example of the problem. As long as housing values continued to rise (and seemed likely to rise indefinitely), the growth of the market in housing derivatives, composed of a huge chain of derivative trades, based on bundling individual mortgages (see chapter 4) seemed to be built on a reasonably positive relationship between the value of homes and the value of housing derivatives, which could sustain an exponentially growing derivative market. In other words, the ratio of housing values to the value of derivatives based on mortgages could be seen as systemic protection against collective risk. But the housing market, as it had to someday, did collapse, and the abilities of various sellers of housing derivatives to find buyers disappeared, creating a freezing of liquidity and a grinding halt to the promise machine.

Each promise made in the great chain of promises represented by the trade in housing derivatives was reasonably valid. But the capacity of the overall system to bear the load of the chain of promises was stressed beyond easy retrieval. This disjuncture has partly to do with the volume of promises creating immense crosscutting promissory chains that were bound to weaken as they became more extended. Worse, every link in the promissory chain was built on greater risk, as distance from the underlying asset was increased. The greater the distance between the two, the larger the gap between the real value of the underlying stock of homes and the overall derivative system based on housing. As risks grew, the housing market became like a toxic version of the Kula ring (Malinowski 1922) in which valuables were traded across a circle of islands in the Pacific to generate both wealth and status by circulating various categories of valuable objects. In the mortgage market in recent years in the United States, traders sought to move their toxic derivatives rapidly to the next buyer, as the inevitable drop in housing values became more imminent. At the end of this chain, when the disaster hit, was the insurance giant, AIG, which in effect was caught holding a massive number of toxic derivatives when the music stopped in 2007.

The conventional wisdom usually lays the blame for the collapse on irresponsible lenders, greedy traders, co-opted rating agencies, and weak regulations. Each of these has some relevance. But at the heart of the collapse of the housing derivatives market, and thus of the financial markets as a whole, was the form of the derivative, which involves piling risk on risk, thus making risk an independent source of profit, with little basis in the realities of production, price, and commodity flows. In a world of derivative assets, money breeds more money, if risks can be bought and sold through securitization, the process by which debts can be bundled, repackaged, and sold time and again. This dynamic, which liberates money almost entirely from Marx's famous formula— M-C-M, allows money to grow, as if magically, on its own, through risk-based credit trading. To understand this development requires a fresh look at the money form, historically the most abstract way in which human beings have reckoned both value and price.

Money and the Language of Derivatives

All the giants of the social science tradition have given thought to money, as a form, a value, and a social fact. Marx's view of money was the key element in his formula about the transformation of money into money through the intermediary of commodities. This formula can well be seen as the first critical effort to understand how money as a form enables the capitalist appropriation of the surplus value of labor, thus allowing capitalist money, in the form of investment in industrial enterprises, to generate and appropriate the bulk of the value of the labor contained in capitalist commodities. Money for Marx is also the key to what he famously discussed as "the fetishism of commodities," that is, the way in which the exchange of commodities under capitalism disguises the social relations that enable its profitable appropriation by capitalists.

Georg Simmel took this line of thinking in another direction, by emphasizing in his famous study of *The Philosophy of Money* (1978) that modern money is the supreme tool of calculation, commensuration, and universalization in the history of humanity, which allows for hitherto-unprecedented and corrosive effects on the bonds between members of society, by allowing impersonal exchange to dominate social relations. But he overlooked risk and the nature of financial capital.

A recent book by Noam Yuran (2014) takes the puzzle about money into a radical new direction by showing how the desire for money needs to be understood. Yuran shows that orthodox neoclassical economics, which appears to be all about money, in fact is built on avoiding the basic question of why money becomes an object of desire. Yuran argues that economics as a discipline is entirely about the uses to which money can be put—to amass goods, power, status, security, or almost anything else—and never addresses why human beings want money *itself*. In other words, economics can never show us why we desire money, and Yuran also argues that to desire money is always to desire more money, that is, that the desire for money, that which is most distant from the desiring subject, thus enables the possibility of desire without limit. This approach to money is not about subjective impulses such as avarice or greed, but reflects the extreme and insoluble alienation that money produces between itself as an object of desire and the desiring human subject. From this point of view, the influential recent study by Michael Sandel (2012), which looks at the limits of commodification in contemporary society by showing how many things once thought to be outside the limits of commodification have become commodities today, asks precisely the wrong question. In the Yuran perspective, Sandel's question presupposes exactly the same axiom as that of neoclassical economics, namely that money is only desired as a means of getting to something else. The mystery is how money comes to be an end in itself, a bottomless magnet for human desire.

The relevance of this debate to my own argument about derivatives trading as a primarily linguistic phenomenon (and the 2007–8 collapse as primarily a linguistic failure) follows Yuran in seeing that money by its nature invites bottomless desire from all human subjects, and that it does so by virtue of its limitless status as an object that cannot be exhausted by the human desire for it. It is possible that money has always had this quality (going as far back as the myth of Midas, which Yuran discusses at length). But it is also clear that the endless capacity of money to attract desire (thus making the desire for money and the desire for *more* money one and the same thing) becomes more evident and generalized as money draws more and more of the social world into its orbit. This expansion is doubtless born in the era of industrial capitalism, when the capacity of money to be used to purchase human labor, machinery, and property of all kinds reaches a new level.

The derivative form takes this bottomless desire for money—itself perhaps a perennial aspect of money—and channels it into instruments that allow money to generate more money without the intervening step of industrial commodity production. In other words, the fact that money itself has no limit, being a manmade symbolic object, finds in the derivative form its highest technical expression. The derivative, which is primarily a way to take a risk on a prior risk, opens the prospect of making money whether the future price of an asset *goes up or down*. This last point is vital, for derivatives traders can make (or lose) money whether underlying prices for assets go up or go down at the end of any particular time interval. This makes risk-taking in the derivatives market independent of the real course of commodity values in the real world of goods and services.

I have already noted that this independence from the movement of prices is already presaged in the commodity futures markets of the mid-nineteenth century, when it became possible to make wagers on future commodity prices without ever acquiring or using the commodities in which trade was occurring. What the contemporary derivative form accomplishes is to make this wager on future prices indifferent to individual risk preferences, to price volatility, and even to the prior history of prices for the asset in question. This is the point at which the heart of the derivative form reveals itself to be a virtually pure linguistic phenomenon, which we might call an *agonistic promise*, a promise to pay the other party if the other party is wrong and you prove to be right about a future commodity price.

An agonistic promise, unlike the pure Austinian promise (discussed earlier) requires two parties whose promises to pay one another have to be simultaneous and mutually exclusive, so that both promises meet the same conditions of felicity though only one of them can be profit-making at the end of the stipulated period of the contract. The second key feature of this sort of agonistic promise is that it depends on the endless tradability of any particular bundle of assets (such bundles are often called securities), something that resembles the endless circulability of money. Failure—or collapse—occurs when the system-wide relations between the buyers and sellers of these assets (measurable by the total dollar value of the derivatives market at any point in time) enter into a crisis because there are no buyers for large amounts of these instruments, thus creating a monumental pile of debt without another buyer left to pick up the mountain of risk now accumulated in the derivatives market.

This is the point in 2008 when the state was forced to come in and buy large amounts of these toxic instruments to artificially jumpstart the financial markets by producing liquidity from its own coffers when no one else was willing or able to do it. At this point, the accelerating and growing chain of performatives ("promises") can grow no further. No one can meet the felicity conditions to make even more agonistic promises, and the situation threatens to collapse on itself, or move backward and downward, exposing the fragility of many of the promises previously made in the building up of this chain. Put another way, what collapsed in 2007–8 was a house of words made of contracts, each contract consisting of an agonistic pair of promises, together composing a performative chain as well as a performative mountain generated by the accrual of money value by the multiplication of wagers on uncertain future prices. When the markets froze, when the music stopped and no buyers could be found for any serious bundle of derivatives, what collapsed was the architecture of promises on which financial profits are composed, in the age of the derivative form.[4]

The argument I have made above—in essence that the failure of the financial promises was at its heart a failure of language—is looked at more closely in the chapters to follow, which begin with a close look at Max Weber's ideas about calculation, salvation, and profit, then move into an examination of Durkheim, Mauss, and the cosmology of the market and the logic of the gift, and conclude with some ideas about failure and mediation, which emerge from this argument about the derivative form and its special role in capitalism today.

CHAPTER TWO

THE ENTREPRENEURIAL ETHIC AND THE SPIRIT OF FINANCIALISM

Max Weber's Problem

This chapter brings me back to my interest in the sociology of economic action, which began for me in 1970 when I first read Max Weber under the baleful eye of the late Edward Shils. It has continued in a series of incarnations: in my doctoral effort to understand the redistributive economies of South Indian temples; in my efforts to look at risk-taking as a historical and cultural formation in a joint project with my friend Chris Bayly in the late 1970s (with the support of the Social Science Research Council); in my research on the measurement epistemologies of farmers in Western India; in my work on the social life of things in the mid-1980s; and, over the last decade, in my research on housing, urban poverty, and the challenges of linking recognition and redistribution as two sides of a navigational capacity which I have described as "the capacity to aspire" (Appadurai 2004). Throughout these decades, I have remained preoccupied with asking why modernization theory and its policy precursor and ally—the field of development economics—had not done better in understanding worldwide processes of economic and cultural transformation. Max Weber has always been with me in these deliberations and I am now finally ready to try to inhabit his thought in a serious way again.

This effort, in my view, does not need massive new data. What is primarily required is a conceptual exercise, a paradigm transformation, a restructuring of existing knowledge: the ingredients for this transformation are available in some key ideas of Max Weber, along with a different reading of some other thinkers, both past and present. The payoff, if the project is successfully completed, is the possibility of creating *a new social science field*—a science of the spirit of calculation—that both combines and transcends approaches currently spread across economics, anthropology and sociology.

Why Weber?

There are many strands of writing that can contribute to my inquiry. I build especially on the work in economic sociology associated with Michel Callon and his many colleagues and collaborators since the 1980s, who have been explicitly indebted to Max Weber and have highlighted the problem of "calculation." But there is relatively little connection between this body of work, which brings together strands in science studies, the sociology of organizations, and economic sociology, and another field of study more centrally concerned with religion, ethics, and salvational ideologies, which includes work on Islamic banking (Maurer 2005); the globalization of the idea of collateral (Riles 2011); the Japanese ethos of arbitrage (Miyazaki 2013);[1] millennial capitalism (Comaroff and Comaroff 2000); genres of the credit economy (Poovey 2008); the link between market logics and American popular religion (Brown 1997); the link between New Age spiritualities and global market discourses (Heelas 2008); the creation of border ethics of profit, taxation, and predation (Roitman 2004); and magic, religiosity, and modernity (Geschiere 1997; Meyer 1999). This second tradition of work is fundamentally concerned with popular understandings of salvation, luck, risk, chance, and divination, and recalls another side of Max Weber's work, which explores uncertainty, proof, and magical action in the domain of commerce, profit, and capital.

In short, Weberian concerns have been taken in two directions, one organizational and technique-centered and the other more concerned with salvational ideologies and techniques of magical wealth-creation. The first may be criticized for an excessive focus on the *mechanisms* of contemporary calculation and the second for an excessive focus on its *ethos*. My intention is to put these two traditions back in live contact to achieve a paradigm shift to study the ethics of calculative action.

The Passions and the Interests

Since the founding period of the social sciences, it has been understood that economic activity has a special ethos and that its institutional transformation usually comes from forces that cannot be explained by economic factors or interests alone. Max Weber's essay on *The Protestant Ethic and the Spirit of Capitalism* (2009) is the *locus classicus* of this conviction, though its roots can be seen in the young Marx and its later expressions, *inter alia*, in the groundbreaking work of Joseph Schumpeter (2008) on innovation.

The problem is this: when the study of patterned human experience (i.e., culture) is institutionally divorced from the study of money, market, and industry, this can create an unproductive divide between our understanding of what Albert Hirschman (1977) called the "passions" and the "interests," and deepen the divide between modern (neoclassical) economics and anthropology, with serious consequences for some of the central questions that face us today. There have been numerous debates and versions of this divide, especially in and around the questions of poverty and development, as well as an honorable series of efforts to close the gap (see Rao and Walton 2004 for an overview of this tradition). But these efforts have yet to put Humpty-Dumpty together again to produce a unified framework for the study of wealth, risk, innovation, and cultural variability. In some regards, especially on the side of economics, the borders have grown harder.

In looking again at the interaction between calculation and redemption, we should also bear in mind that Weber belongs to a distinguished tradition of thinkers, from Pascal to Einstein, all concerned about the role of luck, chance, wager, and probability in human life and divine design. Long considered matters of religion and meaning, these matters are now seen as properties (though often obscure and unintended) of human technology and design.

The key questions for this inquiry fall into two sets. The first set, more general in nature, that remains weakly or partially addressed as a consequence of this divide include the following: (a) Is risk-taking as a proclivity significantly shaped or constrained by cultural presumptions and habits? (b) Are nonmarket behaviors governed by laws as elegant or precise as those that appear to govern the market and, if not, are they measurable only as externalities to market-driven calculation? (c) Is there a systematic way to connect measures of the standard of living to valuations of the quality of life, without making one just a pale shadow of the other? (d) Is there a permanent gap between distributional and relational measures of those goods that human beings appear to seamlessly combine in their sense of "the good life"? (e) Must the ethical considerations that shape economic policy in regard to matters of poverty, justice, and fairness invariably face tradeoffs between theoretical power and descriptive thinness in regard to everyday life? (f) Is calculative action understandable through models of interest, purpose, and strategy that do not obey game-theoretic assumptions, however sophisticated?

Addressing these general questions will also allow clearer answers to a second, more detailed set of questions that come closer to the empirical dynamics of calculative action: (1) Just as some critical elements of Protestant thought facilitated the ethical disciplines and habits that moved forward the calculative ethic of nineteenth-century capitalist entrepreneurs and managers, what sort of ethics can we now identify as facilitating various national and transnational cultures that underpin the massive explosion in leveraging and speculation, in derivative instruments of almost opaque complexity, of financial trading almost completely removed from other forms of property, capital, and assets? (2) How can we reconceptualize the relationship between risk and uncertainty in a world in which catastrophe, emergency, and lack of predictability have made risk itself an object of profit-oriented calculation and speculation, rather than a mere byproduct of natural uncertainties external to the profit-seeking enterprise? (3) What sort of methodicality of spirit, body, and mind can we identify in today's atmosphere of borrowing, leverage, credit, and debt, which unites high-level players and ordinary citizens in many globally linked economies? (4) Is there a reason why the professional callings that underlie the very different fields of accounting and of accountability have lost all links to one another, so that accounting practices now obscure commercial transactions rather than make them more visible and thus accountable to any rational, political, or ethical criterion? (5) Has what Weber called the "spirit of capitalism," which had solid links to trade, manufacture, labor, and profit (as reflected in some sort of balance sheet), given way to an entirely different spirit in which finance has become a magical space, in Weber's sense, rather than an ethical space, where what now counts is profits without known causes and not the methodical rationality of calculation?

Such questions, and others that surround them and follow from them, are of the gravest concern in the world in which we live at the beginning of the twenty-first century, as we face the rapid interdependence of weak fiscal systems, the acceleration of poverty and inequality by most standard measures, and a growing gap between ordinary citizens and those in whom they have placed their economic trust.

Ethic and Ethics

Max Weber is a giant in many traditions of social science inquiry. He falls in a distinguished genealogy of German (and more generally European) thinkers who were incurably curious about major questions of change, structure, cause, and agency in human action. He was in a deep dialogue with great thinkers such as Marx, but also with other major figures from his own lifetime such as Simmel (1978), Brentano

(2011), Sombart (2001), and Troeltsch (1992), who were concerned, in one way or another, with great questions of ethics, economy, power, and history in the German-speaking world in the second half of the nineteenth and early twentieth centuries.

Weber pursued both a systematic and general framework for the study of human societies (an enterprise he never completed to his satisfaction) and a series of empirical studies that encompassed much of the recorded history of the major societies of the world. Of the many questions that preoccupied Weber, none was a bigger source of his ideas and arguments than the question of why modern capitalism of a distinctive sort took shape only in the industrial West. Though others have taken issue with Weber on whether this was a correctly posed question, there is no doubt that it led him to an extraordinary set of conceptualizations, concerning Europe especially, but also about India, China, and the ancient Hebraic world. This question shaped Weber's question with a host of his core ideas, such as the idea of the "calling" (*beruf*), the nature of charismatic leadership, the methodicality of modern capitalist thinking, the character of calculation involved in modern bourgeois entrepreneurship, and the relationship of ethical rationalization to economic rationality of the modern capitalist type. In the process of examining the links between Protestantism, Catholicism, Judaism, Confucianism, and Hinduism (along with other branches and subtraditions within these great religions) and, to a lesser extent, Islam, Weber outlined a set of principles for linking uncertainty, speculation, methodicality, and rationality in the varying configurations that they took in different civilizations and religious traditions at major turning points in time and space.

It is not my interest here to review the detailed, intense, and highly productive debates that these ideas about the comparative study of capitalism have produced in the last century, among economists, scholars of religion and, since World War II, scholars of modernization, development, and economic growth. Nor is it my wish to adjudicate or arbitrate the detailed ways in which the Weberian picture of the great civilizations has been debated, falsified, refined, and enriched in the last century.

Rather, I wish to revisit, reimagine, and redeploy Weber's core ideas about ethics and economics to ask a set of questions about our current global fiscal crises, in hopes of developing a framework that is Weberian in spirit but not necessarily in detail. In other words, this is not an effort to imagine what Weber might have thought or said about the current global economy, but rather to "channel" Weber heuristically. The purpose of this heuristic exercise is *not* to explain some specific contemporary phenomenon (such as outsourcing, or financial derivatives, or post-territorial economic assemblages, or new forms of corporate ethics or governance, or new forms of economic coordination, regulation, and governance) although each of these worthy endeavors is useful in my purposes (LiPuma and Lee 2004; Poon 2008; Sassen 2006).

This framework might cast light on large-scale economic developments in our globalized world by returning to Weber's interests in the ethical underpinnings of calculative action. Ethics, in this usage, are not simply a matter of right and wrong, of deceit or transparency, of honesty or probity, though they may have implications for all of these. Ethics, in the Weberian usage, involves a set of linked understandings of means and ends in the pursuit of calculative action in a world of uncertainty, with a constantly changing set of cultural orientations that inform and shape these understandings. Ethics (in the plural) are always built one ethic at a time, as in Weber's most famous treatise, whose original German title was *Die Protestantische Ethik und der Geist der Kapitalismus* (2009).

The Spirit of Uncertainty

Max Weber used the idea of "*geist*" in a way that has highly specific context in German intellectual history. It deliberately introduced an ideational and idealistic element into the study of the economy, thus creating a direct confrontation with Marx's effort to turn Hegel on his head. Yet, Weber's use of the term *geist* does not succumb to the Hegelian sense of a world spirit moving through history but rather links spirit to a highly local, empirical, and context-specific approach to economic history, which was reflected in Weber's admiration for a series of contemporary Austrian economic historians who did not have much interest in broad dialectical processes; many of them were members of what came to be called the Austrian school of economics.

I suggest that we need to return to the idea of the "spirit" of capitalism, as Weber tried to understand it in *The Protestant Ethic* (2009). Much attention has been paid to the central role, in Weber's understanding of the "spirit of capitalism," to the role of the ideas of vocation, calling, asceticism, methodicality, and sobriety. It is less often remembered that Weber saw this spirit as what enabled the beginnings of modern capitalist enterprise, and as no longer required once capitalism was fully in place as the dominant system of economic organization, commerce, law, and bureaucracy (for a fuller statement of this view see Appadurai 2012).

We cannot afford to see capitalism as a machine that continues to perpetuate itself after an initial ethical moment. Modern capitalism keeps transforming its ethics and the question we need to ask ourselves today is whether we can identify the key elements of the capitalist spirit in today's capitalist environment, almost three centuries after the period in which Weber identified its founding ethical moment. To do so, we can be inspired by Weber but we cannot simply go back to his ideas of methodicality, discipline, vocation, and calling. We need to look again at the nature of capitalist action, especially in the financial sphere, and then ask again what the link between "spirit" and "ethic" might be today. To this end, I suggest the following points of departure.

The *idea of uncertainty* has been almost completely forgotten both by practitioners and analysts who study contemporary capitalism. The overwhelming focus is on "risk." With one striking exception of which I am aware, Beunza and Garud (2006), both economists and sociological students of finance (in both the mechanism tradition and the ethics tradition) have focused on how economic actors experience, manage, calculate, predict, and navigate risk, and hence their biggest technical focus is on probabilistic thinking. Knightian uncertainty has all but vanished from the economy and from its analysis.[2] I propose that we need to look closely at the process, which is simultaneously discursive, technical, institutional, and ideological, by which risk has pushed uncertainty out of the picture, but not entirely successfully. Max Weber, in his study of the Protestant ethic, laid enormous emphasis on uncertainty, not primarily as a technical feature of the economy but as a feature of Protestant religious life, and his entire analysis of the Protestant ethic as a source of capitalist methodicality turned on his analysis of the Calvinist doctrine of *certitudo salutis*, of the certainty of salvation in the face of the radical uncertainty about who was already one of God's elect.

Weber's entire corpus, especially in those writings concerned with the comparative history of capitalism, turned on his particular understanding of the idea of "magic." For Weber, magic was the main obstacle to the birth of Protestant capitalism, the capitalism of methodicality, sobriety, thrift, and discipline. In his lifelong effort to study why other major world religions, such as Hinduism, ancient Judaism, Confucianism, and Taoism, did not have the ethical ingredients to kick-start modern capitalism, the culprit for Weber was "magicality." There have been few thorough efforts to examine how Weber used the word "magic" but my own preliminary study suggests that "magic" for Weber meant some sort of irrational reliance on any sort of technical procedure, in the effort to handle the problems of evil, justice, and salvation. Magic is a kind of coercive proceduralism. Weber, of course, was a great believer in the importance of procedure and associated formalisms in the emergence of modern law, politics, and bureaucracy. But proceduralism in the realm of salvation or ethics was for him a vestige of magical thinking and an obstacle to ethical rationality and methodicality. It is true that Weber did not have a chance to study Catholicism and Islam carefully in his magnificent tour through the world religions, but his passing observations on these cases confirm that he also regarded them as failures in the elimination of magical thinking and the achievement of the clean ethical slate on which Calvinist methodicality might have taken shape.

Today, however, it is possible to identify a series of magical practices (by which I mean both coercive and divinatory performative procedures) at the heart of global capitalism and, in particular, the financial sectors. These practices are premised on a general, absolute, and apparently transcendent faith in the market, which appears both in the daily discourses of traders in the financial markets of this country (as vividly documented recently by Caitlin Zaloom [2006]) and in the plaintive wailings of George W. Bush, when he begged us all to remain loyal members of what I call "the faith-based economy." Reversing the Weberian logic that leads from doubts about salvation, to ascetical discipline, to ethical methodicality, to thrift, and to rational profit-making, the new religion of the market treats the market as the source of certainty, as the reward for disciplined focus on its messages and rhythms, and as the all-powerful force that rewards its own elect, so long as they obey its ethical demands. The magical practices that flow from this faith cover a range of terrains, including: (a) the varieties of what Michel Callon and his colleagues call "formatting" (Callon 1998; Callon, Millo, and Muniesa 2007), which allow no products to be qualified, classified, and made legitimate without necessarily being visible; (b) the role of "framing" in the practices of securities analysts in the face of Knightian uncertainty (Beunza and Garud 2006); (c) the role of finding "likenesses" or similarities in the efforts of investment banks to provide contact languages of valuation for new financial products between sectors of the bank and between the bank and its clients; (d) the multiplex socio-semantic manipulations involved in the evolution of the large class of financial products called "derivatives," all of which have in common the sequences of metonym and metaphor identified long ago as primary properties of magical action; and, (e) the logic of what has been called "financial chartism" (Cetina and Preda 2007) in the technical analysis of financial securities, which explicitly eschews any analysis of fundamentals, that is, of cause-and-effect relationships between prices and other fundamental economic data and instead relies entirely on financial charts of prior price movements, which are used as the basis for predictions of the future. These detailed charts, which are regarded by others as entirely unscientific, have very good standing in financial markets and are in reality no different than the charts of astrologers, psychics, tarot card operators, and other diagrammatic formats for prognostication. In short, they are mechanical techniques of prediction with no interest in causal or explanatory principles. Such examples of magical thinking could be multiplied and detailed across the financial markets in great variety and detail.

Here are some outcomes of the new magicalities that undergird the global financial system and especially its speculative institutions:

The techniques of calculability (and hence its domain) have far exceeded the organizations and tools for its management, hence opening a new distance between expert and popular understandings of risk. I believe that this space is the new location of Knightian uncertainty, and is therefore a magnet for exotic financial products, whose effects on the bottom lines of financial businesses are virtually impossible to measure.

Probability and possibility have become dangerously confused in many popular understandings, thus opening the door to myriad schemes, scams, and distortions based on emergent forms of personal charisma. From the now-infamous hard-luck letters from widows of dictators in West Africa to the charismatic confidence game of Bernie Madoff and Allen Stanford, it is evident that widespread uncertainty is leading to wholesale predation by users of numerical strategies on the gullibility of luck or fortune-oriented thinkers of every variety. The most important space in which to examine the confusion of possibility and probability as ethics, which absorb mass aspirations for change into the space of the official financial sphere, is the burgeoning world of microcredit. I believe microcredit, in its many global incarnations, can be shown to be a space where small-scale savings among the poor are potentially being drawn into large-scale financial profit-making spaces, using the ethicizing discourses of empowerment, trust, and social capital.

The external or transcendent sources of ethics identified by Weber (such as the Calvinist ethic) have been replaced in the corporate world in general, and the financial sector in particular, by various forms of *immanent corporate ethics*, indexed by terms like "transparency," "accountability," "corporate social responsibility," "good governance," and so on, thus making the justification of calculative actions immune from broader ethical images and doctrines.

The single best example of the complexities of immanent corporate ethics is the entire doctrine of *conflict of interest*, which is deserving of much closer study by social scientists. This incarnation of older ideas of corruption, nepotism, and misuse of public office, all of which are offshoots of the modern division between personal and professional interest, are fascinating because of their recursive ethical impossibility. So, if you take a close look at Sarbanes-Oxley, the *locus classicus* of recent legislation calculated to protect individuals and corporations from fraud, you can see that it suffers from the fundamental problem of all ethical voluntarism. It requires self-regulation and self-revelation as guardians against improper business activity and, more specifically, improper profit-making strategies. Close examination of the problems of the doctrine will show that the entire edifice of professional ethics as conceived by Max Weber and others has been exposed as impossible by the financial professions. This opens up a space for a new sort of debate about moral regulation from outside the professional sphere.

Finally, in spite (or perhaps because) of the growth in highly technicalized models of prediction, forecasting, and risk management in the financial sphere, there has been a steady *hybridization of the ideologies of calculative action*, so that the casino, the racetrack, the lottery, and gambling in general have infused the world of financial calculation and vice-versa, thus confusing the spheres of chance and risk as technical features of human life. The examples from India, China, and Japan (discussed in chapter 8) show us the outlines of the hybridization of gambling, astrology, lotteries, gaming, speculation, and day-trading in different societies. Such processes of hybridization have also been remarked in recent studies in the sociology of accounting itself (Miller, Kurunmäki, and O'Leary 2008).

The Calculative Ethos

Let me exemplify my strategy through a preliminary discussion of the word "calculation" itself, a word without which Weber's entire approach to modern capitalism would be impossible to articulate. Though there have been numerous discussions of Weber's ideas about modern bourgeois behavior in the context of Western capitalism, and many efforts to properly understand the meanings of the idea of rationality and the rational in Weber's corpus, there have been no systematic efforts to develop a deep understanding of what Weber might have meant when he used the word "calculation" until very recently. It appears as a key dimension of profit-making behavior, as a key feature of "methodicality" in the Calvinist entrepreneur, as an important dimension of the revolutionary role of double-entry bookkeeping (in Weber's understanding of modern capitalism), and as the primary feature of that ethos which dealt the deathblow to "magic." Magic, for Weber, was the residual element that doomed all the great religious traditions of the world, except for Calvinist Protestantism, to achieve that union of inner and outer methodicality that characterized the "spirit of capitalism."

Today, Max Weber's sense of the importance of "calculation" in human enterprises is hard to recover, as we have overlaid it with a large number of other market-driven ideas, derived largely from the formal developments in neoclassical economics. Thus calculation, in our current scholarly consciousness, is a hazy amalgam of optimization, maximization, choice, quantification, prediction, and agonistic individualism. It is the market, as imaged in our economics textbooks and lodged in our heads, translated into some sort of individual disposition toward people and resources. My preliminary efforts to recover Weber's more capacious and less technical sense of this orientation can be demonstrated by a close look of chapter 22 of Max Weber's *General Economic*

History (2003), translated into English by Frank Knight in 1927. The German original is based on transcriptions of lectures delivered by Weber toward the end of his life, in 1919–20. This lecture is called "The Meaning and Presuppositions of Modern Capitalism" and amounts to an unusually concise version of some of Weber's major ideas on this topic. And in this lecture, the term "calculation" plays a vital role. Consider the opening paragraph of this lecture:

> Capitalism is present wherever the industrial provision for the needs of a human group is carried out by the method of enterprise, irrespective of what need is involved. More specifically, a rational capitalistic establishment is one with capital accounting, that is, an establishment which determines its income yielding power by calculation according to the methods of modern bookkeeping and the striking of a balance. (275)

In this lecture, Weber also goes on to list a series of presuppositions for the existence of "present day capitalism" in which he goes on to state that "capitalistic accounting presupposes rational technology, that is, one reduced to calculation to the largest possible degree, which implies mechanization." Even more interesting, he observes that another characteristic is that of "calculable law," which he elaborates as follows: "The capitalistic form of industrial organization, if it is to operate rationally, must be able to depend upon calculable adjudication and administration." He sums up this dense list of presuppositions and characteristics of Occidental capitalism with a fascinating segue from calculation to speculation:

> To sum up, it must be possible to conduct the provision for needs exclusively on the basis of market opportunities and the calculation of net income. The addition of this commercialization to the other characteristics of capitalism involves intensification of the significance of another factor not yet mentioned, namely specu-

lation. Speculation reaches its full significance only from the moment property takes on the form of negotiable paper. (278)

Even this brief sample of statements surrounding the word "calculation" in a single lecture by Weber offers us a sense of the ways in which calculative behavior had a special set of meanings for him, which extends from the formalization of double-entry bookkeeping and the mechanization of technology, to the predictability of law and administration and speculation based on market opportunity and commercial paper instruments. Here alone, calculation can be parsed into a series of aspects, including formalization, mechanization, predictability, and speculation.

In the next two chapters, I deepen the analysis surrounding risk, uncertainty, and entrepreneurship in Weber's analysis of the Puritan entrepreneur. It is interesting to note that Weber's portrait of the Calvinist entrepreneur emphasizes methodicality rather than risk-taking as a crucial element of his calculative ethic. This is puzzling since Weber certainly understood the role of risk in the history of economics and commerce. What I believe is required is a closer look at the role of the prophet and prophecy in Weber's analysis (where prophets are seen as the charismatic sources of new ethical messages). The question is whether today's financial entrepreneurs, especially those who operate on highly personal reputations and promises, have some of the character of Weber's prophets, and thus allow us to understand better the relationship between prophecy and methodicality in today's financial practices. Put more institutionally and less personally, is the remarkable expansion in instruments for financial risk-taking that characterizes today's global economy in part a product of a renewed charismatic element in the calculative ethics behind today's financial cultures?

Weber's treatment of the idea of calculation, which I discussed briefly, is perhaps the fullest and most systematic of those major early twentieth-century thinkers, including Werner Sombart (2001), Frank

Knight (2009), and Joseph Schumpeter (2008), who were concerned with explaining the key value changes in the world of capitalism.

A recent essay by Peter Miller (2008) draws attention to the critical role of calculation in contemporary debates in the sociology of finance and develops the argument through a close analysis of the role of accounting as a proxy for calculation more generally. I am in full agreement with much of the argument of this essay and see my own arguments as consonant with those of Miller himself, Gordon (1980), Rose (1992), Rose and Miller (2010), Power (1997), and Hacking (1992), all of who are interested in accounting as a technology that underlies many market devices. I am committed to the view that what I call the "ghost in the financial machine" (see chapter 3), which is the spirit behind any specific capitalist ethos or habitus, cannot be derived from the form or arrangement of the devices themselves. This holds for accounting itself, which is itself a meta-device, whose role is to performatively produce the legibility and measurability of other devices, such as the spreadsheet, the flow chart, the proprietary database, and so on. So the ethos of accounting cannot be derived from within its own mechanisms but must be sought within a wider calculative ethos or frame, which is itself historically contingent, and which must be derived from a wider analysis of accounting practices themselves. In this sense this chapter can be seen as a partial response to Miller's well-argued view that the relationship "between ideas of calculation and practices of calculation, or between programmes and technologies" (Miller 2008) needs more work.

Accounting for Uncertainty

The relationship between accounting practices and uncertainty in the financial markets has not been much analyzed or developed. I believe that a close redeployment of Weber's key ideas could be of much use in this sphere, if we accept that the major bridge between economic theories and economic instruments in the contemporary financial world is in the area of uncertainty. Knightian uncertainty remains the major challenge for both theorists and practitioners in the field of finance, and accounts for debates within economics, and between theorists in economics departments and in business schools.

To address the importance of accounting practices in a world of Knightian uncertainty, it is important to return to Weber's analysis of the importance of new accounting practices in the emergence of the modern capitalistic enterprise. In particular, we need to revisit Weber's idea of "capital accounting," one of the most lucid expositions of this fundamental innovation in the history of capitalism.

This analysis of the historical role of capital accounting permits us to make a critical link between Weber and Knight on the matter of uncertainty. Weber's analysis of capital accounting shows that without an innovative accounting device, which permitted capital accounting, there could be a growth in the wealth of an actor, but there could be no profit. Let me quote Weber (1978) on the idea of profit:

> There is a form of monetary accounting which is peculiar to rational economic profit-making; namely, "capital accounting." Capital accounting is the valuation and verification of opportunities for profit and of the success of profit-making activity by means of a valuation of the total assets (goods and money) of the enterprise at the beginning of a profit-making venture, and the comparison of this with a similar valuation of the assets still present and newly acquired, at the end of the process; in the case of a profit-making organization operating continuously, the same is done for an accounting period. (91)

This observation leads Weber to say that "an economic enterprise (*Unternehmen*) is autonomous action capable of orientation to capital accounting" (92). Furthermore, Weber observes, in a crucial passage, that in a market economy "every form of rational calculation, especially of capital accounting, is orientated to expectations of prices and their changes" and this form of calculation depends critically on double-entry bookkeeping (92). Thus accounting is a precondition to the very idea of profit, and is very far from a mere method of recording or measuring something which exists prior to the practice of double-entry book keeping. Here, Weber has already identified the primary idea behind the entire corpus of MacKenzie and Callon on economic performativity, in spite of their later debates and refinements of this insight. Nevertheless, as I argue in more detail in the next chapter, Weber barely paid any attention to risk, and his interest in uncertainty was wholly focused on the salvational uncertainty of the Calvinist Protestant believer. This is where Frank Knight comes in.

Frank Knight's classic work on risk and uncertainty (2009) is enjoying a revival in economics, finance, and sociology, but there is still very little progress on how to take up the analysis of Knightian uncertainty. A recent essay by a distinguished economist and financial practitioner is a strong reminder that we will all fail to explain the current financial crisis until we face Frank Knight's blunt observations about uncertainty to the effect that "profit arises out of the inherent, absolute unpredictability of things, out of the sheer, brute fact that the results of human activity cannot be anticipated and then only in so far as even a probability calculation in regard to them is impossible and meaningless" (Knight, quoted in Janeway 2006).

William Janeway (2006) makes a strong argument to the effect that no amount of manipulation of current models and strategies for managing or forecasting risk will solve the problem of Knightian uncertainty, and reminds us that Knight was deeply aware that the problem of uncertainty was a product of the fact that the economy was a forward-looking process and that, in the words of Paul Davidson (1994), the economy was a nonergodic system. We also need to notice that Frank Knight was the first major thinker to recognize that uncertainty was the critical site in which profit-making activity found its success or failure, rather than in the sober methodicality of the Weberian businessman.

In a brilliant essay by Maria Brouwer (2003), she juxtaposes the ideas of Weber, Schumpeter, and Knight on the role of entrepreneurship in economic development, and demonstrates both the dialogue and the differences between these three major thinkers, and distinguishes the Weberian entrepreneur, Schumpeter's innovator, and Knight's risk-financing capitalist, the latter being the only one who selects among alternative innovative ideas in the face of uncertainty. Brouwer is thus able to show the direct linkage of profits to uncertainty; the brilliance of Knight's insight that it is finance that makes the crucial difference in determining which innovations will actually come to market, and how the capacity of the financier to take risks on specific innovations actually depends on the capacity to face uncertainty rather than to manage risk. Profit is the reward for facing uncertainty, and not for managing risk or even less, as in Weber's analysis, for methodical business practice.

What Brouwer misses is that if we go back to Weber's ideas about the centrality of capital accounting to profit-making, as opposed to his picture of the sober Puritanical businessman, we can see that Weber did understand the priority of the Calvinist ethos of profit-making (as opposed to wealth acquisition) to their new use of the existing instruments of double-entry bookkeeping, which were in fact designed to measure the relationship between current and future asset value. In this sense, Weber did see that accounting was a tool for managing expectations. What has confused many later analysts, including myself, is our tendency to confuse the charismatic confidence of Calvin himself (in his certainty of grace and thus in his endorsement of the organization of all of life to the glory of God, beyond the confinement of the monastic life) with the more systematic, methodical, rationalized profile of his Puritan followers. The inner certainty, the ecstatic confidence, and the irrational sense of election are all characteristic of Calvin and, suitably recontextualized and articulated, the key to today's short sellers and bears that have no risk-managing devices on which to rely.

So where does this leave a new approach to the relationship between accounting, uncertainty, and the financial market? If the entire apparatus of probabilistic devices for probabilistic forecasting cannot be any sort of profit-making in the face of uncertainty (or wagering on one's own sense of the direction and the timing of the downturn in the case of short sellers), we might need to look again at the innovations on the accounting side of the financial markets as the key devices that have now become guides for the exploitation of uncertainty. This possibility has been touched on in recent studies of the performativity of new accounting protocols.

My own (still to be fully developed) intuition is that the spirit that informs today's heroic, charismatic players at the very high ends of the financial market lies not in an as-yet-undiscovered set of proprietary databases, screens, tools, or models, to which lesser players in the market do not have access. Rather, these are players who have a different strategy of divination, of reading the signs, charts, trends, flows, patterns, and shifts in the market than those who are less willing to take their outsize bets on the certainty and timing of market downturns. The sources of this divinatory confidence are what need exploration in a separate context, by thinking through the right sites, narratives, and reports from which to glean this data.

Cultures of Calculation

The larger challenge, to which this chapter is partly an open invitation, is to create the scaffolding for a new field of social inquiry, which builds on a century of dialogue between economists, anthropologists, and sociologists. It seeks to break out of existing mutual biases about methodology to create a vocabulary that might help us to build, in Weber's spirit, a general theory of calculative action. In using the term "calculative action," I index a set of concepts, methods, and questions that could help to inaugurate a unified field of inquiry, focused on calculative action as a central feature of twenty-first-century economies. While it would be premature to say too much about what the principles and methodological profile of this field of inquiry would be, it is important to say that it would draw, in spirit, on various strands in development economics; on the anthropology of markets, finance, and religion (Comaroff and

Comaroff 2000; LiPuma and Lee 2004; Miyazaki 2007; Riles 2001, 2004, 2011; Zaloom 2006); on the social science of new religiosities (Guyer 2007; Heelas 2008; Maurer 2005); on behavioral economics (Levitt and Dubner 2005; Schelling 1978); and on the psychology of lay reasoning, choice, and error (Kahneman and Tversky 1979); and, above all, on recent science studies and social studies of finance (Beunza and Stark 2004; MacKenzie 2006; MacKenzie, Muniesa, and Siu 2007; Poon 2008).

Developing such a science of calculative action will require economists to put history and culture back into the study of calculative action, since the single greatest failing of neoclassical economics is its self-enclosing conviction that models of the market are always the best way to understand the ethos of the market. It will also require anthropologists, in particular, to take as much account of the ways in which persons, institutions, and leaders, in different cultural settings, go about the business of making their futures, understood always as cultural designs for the good life, as they have of history, tradition, custom, and habit in shaping human orientations. Economists who wish to join forces in building this new space of inquiry will have to forsake the virtues of parsimony and formal elegance to look again at the historical and cultural details of the real economies in which both wealth and poverty are produced. In moving in these directions, we will bring back not only the spirit of Max Weber, but also a host of other great thinkers about the economy (from Marx and Brentano to Sombart and Schumpeter) who refused to separate the *oikos* from the rest of culture and society and calculation from its ethical and cultural underpinnings.

CHAPTER THREE

THE GHOST IN THE FINANCIAL MACHINE

This chapter circles back to Max Weber through an engagement with Marcel Mauss. My starting point is Derrida's famous argument about the "impossibility" of the gift, which annuls itself by its implicit expectation (a negative performative) of a return. I focus here on the idea of the "return" as a device for deepening the argument about the derivative logic of contemporary financial devices.

Derrida's argument about the logical impossibility of the pure gift is in fact anticipated in the very first pages of Mauss's classic essay on *The Gift* (1990), in the perception by Mauss of the inner contradiction between the voluntary and the compulsory and the disinterested and the self-serving elements of the category of the gift. Two facts about Mauss's study have been lost from view. One is that his entire and fundamental interest throughout this essay is in the question: what is the force behind *the obligation to return*? The second point, which Mauss also makes clear, is that his thorough archaeology of the gift (in both primitive and archaic societies) was wholly motivated by his interest in the moral force behind the modern contract (legal, impersonal, and obligatory). Bearing these two points in mind allows us to understand better what may have been Mauss's rich and only partial answer to his question, which was that the obligation to return lay in the spirit of the thing given (the famous *hau* of Polynesia), which in turn provided a dynamic and forceful connection between giver and receiver, and the first giver and the second giver/returner, and so forth.

I draw two conclusions from this reading of Mauss. The first is that Mauss was quite aware of the inner affinity between archaic and modern forms of binding by giving. And he was interested in the "spirit" behind the archaic gift, which he was also convinced was the "spirit" behind the modern contract. This spirit had to do with a series of cosmologies (themselves dramatically different), all of which see some things as imbued with the spirit of the giver and thus capable of exercising a moral force on the receiver. This spirit is what animates the specific devices or forms taken by the gift. Notice here that his sociological strategy is to induce the spirit not from the device but from some other nonmechanical source. This sense of spirit closely resembles Max Weber's notion of the "spirit" of capitalism, by which usage Weber sought to capture the spirit, the anima, behind specific capitalist forms and devices (such as double-entry bookkeeping and rational calculation of profit).

Both Mauss and Weber stand on one side of a great divide that we also see around us today. On the one side, we have Michel Callon and his many colleagues and collaborators (Latour, MacKenzie, Beunza, Stark, and many others) who argue that the best way to understand new economic devices, especially the devices of the market, is to account for their performativity as devices.[1] On the other side stand thinkers like Mauss and Weber (but also others like Boas, Schumpeter, and Hirschman) who argue that there is something akin to a Godel-type problem in inducing the spirit that animates a particular set of mechanisms from within the properties of the device itself. The rest of the chapter is an extension of this "animistic" argument and its relevance to modern financial markets.

The Spirit in Weber

I looked closely at Weber's parsing of the ideas of "calculation" and "spirit" in chapter 2. I return now to look more closely at his use of the word "spirit" (*geist*), most famously in his essay on *The Protestant Ethic and the Spirit of Capitalism* (2009), a usage that has nowhere clearly been analyzed. It belongs to a family of Weberian terms, which include "ethic," "ethos," and "habitus." This last word, most often seen as part of our debt to Pierre Bourdieu, has been noticed by Jean Pierre Grossein (1996), whose translation into French of some of Weber's key writings on religion might be one key to the relationship between Weber and the work of Bourdieu and his collaborator Passeron. The other is Bourdieu's explicit debt to Mauss, who was the first modern user of the term "habitus."

"Spirit" in Max Weber's usage is most often read as belonging to the nineteenth-century sense of the German word *geist*, and is thus assumed to refer to the worldview of an epoch or historical age. This is not wholly wrong and Weber's own use of the word "ethos," which is related to his use of the word "spirit," refers to a cultural sensibility, associated with a group, class, profession, or sect, which is more diffuse than a mere ideology or doctrine, and conveys a sense of a disposition, a sensibility, a moral style, and elements of a cultural psychology. In this sense, when Weber speaks of the spirit of capitalism, he does not mean its explicit doctrines, its ideology, or even its specific technical orientations to market, profit, and calculation. He means something less formal, more dispositional and moral, something that also makes sense of its crystallization in a particular "ethic."

As Weber, in *The Protestant Ethic* (2009), sets out to describe the spirit of capitalism, he embarks on an interesting methodological exercise in which the key elements of the "spirit" of capitalism lie outside its technical or professional expressions and speak to a disposition which is somehow anterior (both logically and historically) to its concrete calculative expressions in nineteenth-century capitalist behavior. This anterior "ethos" begins to anticipate Bourdieu's use of the term "habitus," a term that was familiar to Weber himself. Various scholars have touched on the links between the ideas of style, deportment, disposition, and spirit in Weber's corpus.

If we look at spirit in this way, as a matter of disposition rather than worldview, it comes closer to an embodied moral sensibility, which precedes action or organization and amounts to a collective psycho-moral disposition. In this sense, the "spirit" of capitalism, in Weber's argument, is external to and prior to any and all of its distinctive devices, both technological and institutional. The content of this spirit is what will lead us back to Mauss's thoughts on the gift.

Weber's discussion of the "spirit" of capitalism in chapter 2 of his famous essay (2009) demands a close rereading.

Animating Modern Capitalism

After a close reading of a series of extracts from two famous works of Benjamin Franklin, Weber notes, "In fact, the *summum bonnum* of this ethic, the earning of more and more money, combined with the strict avoidance of all spontaneous enjoyment of life, is above all completely devoid of any *eudaemonistic,* not to say, hedonistic, admixture" (2009, 53). Weber goes on to suggest that all varieties of avarice, of adventurism, of reckless pursuit or profit, are not part of the Franklin ethos. He further goes on to say that the most plausible answer (before his own) was that of Werner Sombart, who argued that the spirit of modern capitalism lay in the gradual emergence of rationalization.

Weber gives Sombart much credit but argues, in a few closely reasoned pages (75–78) that rationalization is by itself an inadequate source for the modern spirit of systematic, even ascetical, commitment to moneymaking. In fact, he suggests that the spirit of modern capitalism actually has something "irrational" about it that requires historical sourcing and that this irrationality is in fact expressed in the hostility of the Franklin ethic to the eudaemonistic motive for moneymaking. This irrational component is what leads Weber to the Protestant conception of the "calling" as the key to the modern spirit of capitalism. In chapter 3 of *The Protestant Ethic* (2009), he does a close reading of Luther's conception of *beruf* (calling) and shows that it is in fact too traditionalistic to be the source of the spirit of Franklin: that is, it was still an attitude to worldly activity that was cautious and qualified, because of

Luther's antipathy to any disposition that might lead back to the doctrine of "salvation through works." This step leads Weber to argue that to truly find the source of Franklin's irrational restraint about money-making we must turn to Calvin and his ideas about election, proof, and salvation.

Weber's reading of Calvin, which is the pivot of *The Protestant Ethic* (2009), is contained in chapter 4, which has the title "The Religious Foundations of This-Worldly Asceticism." Every line of this chapter has been read and debated, both in Weber's own lifetime and up to the present day. So I will note just one critical element of what Weber found in Calvin, which he thought distinguished Calvin from Luther and was the key to Weber's argument about the "spirit" of modern capitalism. This is the spirit of "methodicality." Chapter 4 of *The Protestant Ethic* is virtually a thriller, a heart-stopping effort to trace a key distinction, to get to the heart of a mystery, to catch a great idea in its germinal form. It has a breathtaking urgency about it, a break-neck attention to the trail, and a remarkable lateral attention to possible alternative paths, which need to be rejected or avoided.

We see here a series of careful efforts by Weber, mainly to distinguish Calvin's views on grace, works, election, and proof, both from earlier Catholic views and from Luther's views, which come close to the later Calvinist position and then retreat from it. The drift here is toward taking the ascetical (monastic) model of systematic ethical action and moving it into a model for the systematic ethical organization of the totality of a man's life. Weber points out that the plight of Calvin's believer is that as a consequence of his belief in God's power, grace, and fore-ordained plan for man's salvation there is no way whatsoever for man to intercede, either by prayer, by confession, or by works to God's decision about who is saved and who is not. Furthermore, there is no way to *distinguish* by their behavior or by any other sign those who are saved from those who are not. This produces an immense form of loneliness (here Weber is very much in the line of Kierkegaard) and the systematic and methodical dedication of one's life to the accumulation of wealth is only a sign to oneself of a life that resembles the sort of life that can enhance God's glory, regardless of whether one is or is not one of the elect. This pattern of life is not intended as an effort to influence God in any way (for that is absurd in Calvin's theology), nor is it a sign of inner certainty about one's own status. It is in fact a *gamble on God's grace*. But it is a special sort of gamble. It is not a gamble on an outcome. It is a *derivative gamble*: that is, it is a gamble on a gamble. The primary gamble is a gamble on the possibility that one is one of the elect (already predetermined but absolutely unknowable); the second is the gamble that in performing as if one is one of the elect, one is likely to be acting to enhance the glory of God, that is, as one who is not one of the elect but is nevertheless performing as if one was saved.

One could make a cruder reading of Weber's interpretation of Calvin to the following effect. I can never know if I am one of the elect. This makes me feel lonely and anxious. So I will act as if I am one of the elect, by dedicating my *worldly* life to a methodical ethical plan. This will change nothing. But it will make me feel better because, at the very least, I am acting to celebrate God's grace in my own way. A more nuanced reading would be that the Calvinist approach to profit-making in this world—absent any possibility of certainty about one's status as saved or damned—is as a derivative gamble in the face of radical uncertainty, about the disposition of God's grace. That is, Calvinist economic methodicality in the pursuit of worldly wealth (ascetical rationality) is a gamble on the felicity of a performative.

Risk and Grace in Weber

The stage is now set to discuss the biggest puzzle in looking at Weber's work on the entrepreneurial ethic and indeed his work on economic history more generally: it contains virtually no references to the problem of "risk," except in some brief asides on medieval shopping and commerce, in his famous study of general economic history (Weber 2003). This is a bit surprising since Weber's ideas about the emergence of modern capitalism remain among the major arguments about the "entrepreneurial" spirit in the nineteenth and twentieth centuries.

A close reading of *The Protestant Ethic* (2009) and Weber's other writings on what he often called "ascetical capitalism" reveal two things that cast light on this puzzle. The first is that Weber's primary ideas about uncertainty were expressed in his account of Calvin's ideas about grace, election, and salvation, and the profound uncertainty (hence the loneliness) of the Calvinist believer, who could never look into the black box of divine providence to ascertain whether or not he was one of the saved. This radical uncertainty, which leads to the doctrine of *certitudo salutis* (the certainty of grace), was at the very heart of Weber's account of the Calvinist ethos. When it comes to modern capitalism and its spirit, Weber puts his entire stress on the linked ideas of "methodicality," rationalization, calculation, and sober business practice. Nowhere in his account of ascetical capitalism is risk mentioned, even when he focuses on profit as the critical expression of double-entry bookkeeping and capital accounting in modern commercial organizations. Weber's quintessential Calvinist is not a risk-taker. Or, more precisely, it was not the risk-taking side of modern business enterprises that most interested Weber.

Prima facie, this fact seems to disqualify Weber from being invoked in any discussion of the contemporary financialization of capitalism, since this process has risk at its very heart. What then can we take from Weber, given his complete disinterest in risk as a feature of the modern entrepreneurial enterprise? To answer this question, we must take a page out of Weber's own book and note that he did not say that the Calvinist spirit was crucial to the ongoing, routinized evolution of capitalism but only to its originary moment (that moment that he identified more in the eighteenth than in the nineteenth century). After that moment capitalism becomes a self-propelling machine that no longer requires the ascetical spirit of capitalism in order for its key players to be animated and motivated. The Calvinist spirit, in this later phase, has been fully incorporated into the capitalist machine. This methodological division between the founding moment and later moments is a distinction I will return to make again in regard to risk.

Put more precisely, I would like to argue that the period since the early 1970s (which might be seen as the beginning of the thoroughgoing financialization of capitalism, especially and initially in the United States) is not in fact a moment of unbridled risk-taking, as so many analysts and media observers have been prone to say, especially in the wake of the 2009 global meltdown. I would suggest rather that it is a period when *the spirit of uncertainty* has been reawakened in relation to the unprecedented formalization/abstraction/commercialization of the machinery of risk itself.

So here is the proposition I think is worthy of careful further development and critique. In the course of the last half-century (but especially since 1970 or so), the machinery for measuring, modeling, managing, predicting, commoditizing, and exploiting risk has become the central diacritic of modern capitalism. Financial markets lead and shape other markets, financial capital vastly outstrips manufacturing or industrial capital, financial policymakers dominate global economic policy, and major economic crises are produced and prolonged by the runaway growth of risk instruments, markets, and creative legal and accounting devices. The careful sociological analysis of these devices is the greatest accomplishment of the major scholars working on the sociology of finance (Callon, MacKenzie, Stark, and their numerous colleagues and collaborators). The bulk of this work, and corresponding technical work within the finance field itself comes out of the path-breaking work by F. H. Knight on risk and uncertainty (2009). The following extract from the Wikipedia entry on Knight captures the essence of Knight's breakthrough:

> Knight invented the notion of what has come to be called Knightian uncertainty, where he made a distinction between risk and uncertainty. He argued that situations with risk were those where decision making was made faced with unknown outcomes but known ex-ante probability distributions. He argued that these sit-

uations, where decision making rules such as maximizing expected utility can be applied, differ in a deep way from those where the probability distribution of a random outcome is unknown. While most economists today would recognize the difference between the two situations, there has been little progress in terms of writing models and doing empirical tests of problems with Knightian uncertainty.[2]

Although there is some emerging work in economics on "Knightian uncertainty" it is not yet easily available or widely discussed in the literature on the sociology of finance,[3] which is largely preoccupied with risk-based measures and practices. I look forward to an emerging future dialogue in which work on Knightian uncertainty (as opposed to risk) can provide a new platform for conversations between sociologists, economists, and anthropologists concerned with modern finance.

Meanwhile, it is interesting to note that Frank Knight, the father of all subsequent work on the economics of risk, was also a major American translator and mediator of Weber and that he saw much to commend in Weber's work in economic history. Absent any explicit discussion (of which I am aware) by Frank Knight of Weber's views of the capitalist spirit, I propose the following argument.

Risk is now part and parcel of the machinery of contemporary capitalism, and the "devices" that measure, model, and forecast risks are central to the financialization of modern capitalism. What has happened to Knightian uncertainty (apart from the famous Rumsfeldian formulation about "knowing what we don't know")? We might say that while some actors in the field of finance do know what they don't know, and perhaps also what they would like to know, they certainly have no good way to measure what they don't know, and even more, they don't know how to measure it probabilistically. Thus uncertainty remains outside all financial devices and models. So what do we, as analysts, do about uncertainty in the current financial world? I suggest that a set of attitudes, dispositions, intuitions, in short an ethos (or what we might today call an imaginary) about uncertainty is certainly discernable and it cannot be directly deduced from any social or technical study of practices in which risk devices are embedded. In what does this imaginary consist?

The Uncertainty Imaginary

Max Weber found the ethos of rational capitalist action in the Calvinist mindset, in a specific set of ideas about God's grace, human salvation, the nature of proof about election to the company of the saved, and the bourgeois virtues that this set of ideas engendered, which he labeled "ascetical capitalism." Plainly, when we look at the heroes (and demons) of the last forty years in global finance, especially in the United States (individuals such as Milliken, Bosky, and Madoff), we cannot see in them much of the spirit of the ascetical Calvinist businessmen who was deeply opposed to greed, excess, exuberance, and worldly pleasure in almost any form. Rather, the typical "master" of the financial universe is not a dull or nerdy accountant or lawyer but a gaudy, adventurous, reckless, amoral type who embodies just the sort of avarice, adventurism, and charismatic self-motivation that Weber saw as the absolute enemy of systematic capitalist profit-making.

It is not hard to see, especially in the last year or two, when we look at the extraordinary incomes, extravagant lifestyles, and swashbuckling heroics of the major bankers, hedge-fund managers, arbitragers, swappers, insurers, and their wannabe juniors, that we are in the presence not of sober risk-managers but of individuals who have chosen to define, without any models, methods, or measurements to guide them, the space of financial uncertainty as such. In this regard, these heroes of the financial imaginary are precisely not about the taming of the "passions" by the "interests" (in Hirschman's famous formulation) but are rather about the animation of the interests by the passions.

That is, the world of financial risk, and its numerous emerging instruments and devices, is in fact nothing other than an enormous set of tools, a technology, for the mapping and measuring of risk, not in order to manage it but rather in order to *exploit* it. But the exploitation of risk, by definition, cannot be animated within the boundaries of the information provided to any player by his or her devices alone. It is of course clear that financial players also use information gathered from their peers, their social networks, the media, and, not least, their prior worldly experiences. But the availability of such extra-technical information is a truism. What is important is the ethos, the spirit, the imaginary through which the world of the screen, the floor, the office, and even the invisible collegial network is valued, assessed, and shaped. Markets may be about efficiency but financial actors are not. Nor will individualistic psychological theories of expectation, preference, utility (which constitute 99% of the foundation of behavioral economics) take us any further, for we are interested in collective orientations and dispositions.

I propose that the primary features of the ethos of financial players in the last few decades, those who have both played and shaped the financial game, is to be found in a working (though not consciously theorized or articulated) disposition towards uncertainty as a legitimate principle for reintroducing risk into the milieu of uncertainty. In other words, those players who define the strategies through which financial devices are developed and operated (as opposed to those who simply react or comply with these strategies) use their own intuitions, experiences, and sense of the moment to outplay other players who might be excessively dominated by their tools for handling risk alone. In short, these key players (the contemporary incarnations of Benjamin Franklin, John Baxter, and so on, in Weber's argument) are those who are not just bold enough and wealthy enough to "sell short" (for example), like John Paulson and George Soros, but also those who are in one or other way skeptical of the reliability of devices. This group includes, but is not confined to, short sellers.

The ethic of what we may call "device skeptics" in today's financial world is not yet easy to glean, even with the plethora of narrative accounts of the great players and dramas in the financial markets of recent years (viz. Cohan 2009; Lewis 2010; Morris 2008; Tett 2009; Wessel 2010; Zandi 2008). Still we can suggest some possibilities for characterizing this type of actor. First, they are not afraid to be pessimistic about the possibilities of certain markets, economies, and even nations. Second, they are "contrarian" in their approach to most general opinions about investment and stock appreciation. Third, they are willing to take large bets on their pessimistic assessment of weak corporations, bad underwriting, and current credit rating consensus. The common structural property of each of these dispositions is simple: their sense of the environment of relevant uncertainties inclines them to be more confident about their reading of downside rather than of upside risks. If it is true that whatever rises must fall, and that whatever falls must rise (virtually the founding axiom of the financial markets), the short-sell ethic or imaginary is more comfortable with the inevitability of fall. This might be described as the core of the imaginary of uncertainty. We might suggest that those financial players who are inclined to sell short, due to a sort of structural pessimism, are more confident about downside than about upside risk. This is clearly tied to the major feature that distinguished short sellers who make money (even fortunes) rather than losing money, which is their confidence in their capacity to be right about the *timing* of the downturn. This is the key to large profits on the short sell. Thus, these are players who are not only contrarians but are actors who are willing to infuse their reading of uncertainties (doubtless hard to quantify) into their reading of the timing of the downturn as measured on the screens that reflect risk.

I am not here trying to privilege "bears" over "bulls" or pessimists over optimists in the financial markets. I am interested in those who are willing to recognize that the main brute fact about uncertainty is that it might not favor you in the management of risk. Their pessimism is at least as exemplary of the imaginary of uncertainty as the ethos of those who consistently bet on short- or long-term upswings in any financial market. Contrarians define a tendency to wager on uncertainty rather than on risk as such. This is my hypothesis about the spirit of those actors that defines the financialization of contemporary capitalism.[4]

The question that remains to ask is what the spirit (ethos, ethic) that underpins the ethos of these "bears" might be. Here I turn to the work of Jackson Lears (2003) on the historical tension between the culture of chance and the culture of control in American history. In this brilliant work, Lears documents the deep interconnections between religion, commerce, and leisure in American life, as well as the multiple historical sources of this tension. He suggests that today's speculators and day-traders represent the still-powerful yearning among Americans for the undeserved victory, the lucky gamble, which animates parts of the American economy, and argues that this ethos is part of the deep belief in grace, outside of all human efforts, that still animates many Americans.

I see much of merit in Lears's argument, not least his readings of Mauss and Weber. However, I propose one significant modification of his account. In my view, the masters of the financial universe, particularly those who have the confidence in their own capacity to be lucky in the timing of the short sell, are not really acting on their faith in the workings of chance to offset the working of systems of control. Rather, they believe in their capacity to channel the workings of chance to win in the games dominated by cultures of control. More precisely, they believe in their capacity to channel the workings of uncertainty to be winners in games of risk. All the instruments of risk that characterize today's financial markets (most important, the modern derivatives such as over-the-counter derivatives, unregulated by any clearinghouse) are "devices" whose buying and selling are available to anyone with the resources to purchase them. But selling them short requires a deep confidence in the realm of Knightian uncertainty, where there are, by, definition no tools for either modeling or forecasting the timing of the downturn. This confidence, whatever its sources, is the "grace" that the most powerful bears believe they possess.

It is not at all obvious that this sort of belief in the grace that allows one to infuse the machinery of risk with the spirit of chance among today's leading bears is a matter of religion, culture, or class, in any simple sense. Such individuals come from many religious, cultural, and national backgrounds and indeed do not have even hold common political values (note the contrast between George Soros and John Paulson, for example). So it does not make sense to replicate the Weberian answer and identify some sort of religious ethos as the distinctive feature of the disposition of these actors. It remains an important ethnographic challenge to identify the contours of this ethic of grace, which in these players takes the form of a capacity to channel uncertainty so as to tame the machinery of risk.

One possible objection to my proposal needs to be addressed: my approach to the ethic that animates the machinery of today's financialized capitalism takes as its quintessential players the bears, the contrarians, the short sellers. Does this not put players who are by definition against the herd at the center of the sociology of finance? Can outliers be modal social types? My tentative answer is that in a historical moment when the exploitation of risk for the maximization of profit is the central feature of the reigning game, those who are willing to bet against the majority are even better exemplars of the general ethos than those who are fully committed to the general wisdom about growth, upticks, secular improvements, and eternal self-correction in a market that comes closer and closer to complete efficiency. The players who are most revealing of the foundational ethos in such a context are not those who wish to "tame chance" but those who wish to use chance to game the otherwise deterministic play of risk.

Mauss and the Problem of Return

This long excursus into a Weberian reading of the ethos of today's financialized capitalism was initiated by some reflections on Mauss. I now return to these reflections. Mauss's key idea—which was intended to explain not just the logic of gifts in archaic and primitive economies but also the spirit of the contract in modern societies—was that the obligation to return was animated by the spirit of the gift, which was in turn produced by the entwinement of giver, gift, and receiver in the spirit of the thing. In Mauss's analysis, one form of this logic was to be found in Polynesia, and the other form, much more competitive, political, and aggressive, was to be found in the potlatch ceremonies of the American Northwest, most richly analyzed by Franz Boas. Mauss's analysis of the North American potlatch viewed it as an intermediate form between the entirely reciprocal, collective, and totalizing spirit of the gift economy and the individualizing, utilitarian, and impersonal ethos of the modern contractual economy. Hence the potlatch tended to revolve around themes of honor and credit, which were less marked in the gift economies of Polynesia. The high-status players in the potlatch were willing to spend, give away, and burn great amounts of property (blankets, food, and coppers) in efforts to make the reciprocal gift a difficult one and to create temporary status inferiority for the recipients of their excess gifts. The ethos of the potlatch is the ethos of the destructively large wager, the aggressively excessive gift. In gambling terms, this is an "all-in," a wager of "everything." The expectation of return in the potlatch is predicated on a downward spiral of excessive gifts, a kind of mutually assured destruction over time that binds all players in the game.

This form of agonistic giving is also part of the spirit of the large short sellers who bet on the size and timing of major downturns in the market. While such short sellers are often criticized for betting on failure in specific corporations, markets and even national economies, they are also lauded for doing the diligence that identifies weak assets and overvalued corporations well before the general population. Such short sellers are also taking large bets predicated on a series of downturns, in which their chance of big returns is based on placing big bets on a downward spiral. When John Paulson buys insurance on large bundled sets of toxic subprime mortgages (through Goldman Sachs and others) he is betting on the obligation of return to him when the inevitable downturn occurs. Those who buy his bundles of subprime mortgages are also compelled by the obligation to return.

Thus, there is a simple way to get from Mauss's ideas about the potlatch to today's contrarians and short sellers. The players in the traditional Northwest American potlatch are classical examples of a willingness to bear high risks for high returns. So are their counterparts who specialize in the short sell. The difference is that today's financial players are able to take advantage of Frank Knight's work and use their sense of grace (in regard to uncertainty) to animate their manipulation of derivative markets and their risk devices. They too rely on being successful beneficiaries of the power of the devices they operate to guarantee returns that are quite disproportionate to the amounts they wager to begin with. Especially in the world of today's hedge funds, what is at stake, exactly as Mauss pointed out for the potlatch, are the interlinked nature of honor and credit.

The Ghost in the Machine

It remains now to explain the title of this chapter. A serious effort to look at various critical breaks, shifts or innovations (such as double-entry bookkeeping, subprime mortgages or shareholder value, among others) presents opportunities to the hypothesis, directly derived from Weber, that the "spirit" of capitalism can exist without any clear institutional, technical or organizational expression for it; and that, conversely, practical forms of capitalism can be identified absent the "spirit," as Weber described it (see especially chapter 2 of The Protestant Ethic [2009]). Relaxed somewhat, what this line of thinking suggests, for example, is that the multitude of today's market devices (in Callon's sense) can be hypermethodical (quantified, monitor-able, external, and impersonal) while the spirit of their operators could be avaricious, adventurous, exuberant, possessed, charismatic, excessive, or reckless in the manner that Weber argued was exactly not the spirit of modern capitalism. In other words, if "spirit" and "system" change over time but often without reference to one another, today's financial world might be a moment of maximum disjuncture (or torque) between hypercharismatic leaders and hypermethodical devices. There are, of course, other less simple combinations and conjunctures, but to explore any of them requires us to admit the gap between the "ghost" and the" machine," each of which might change relatively independently but together define the nature of the "system" as an empirical complex at any given place/time.

In a sense, this hypothesis opens an internal tension in the tradition of science and technology studies that was massively shaped by Bruno Latour and Michel Callon, and evolved into the general form of actor network theory (ANT). This powerful theory itself contains two contradictory impulses. Bruno Latour brilliantly formulates one in his book on the dynamic role of "assemblages" in the constitution of the social (2005). The other is expressed in many of Callon's writings on the nature and sociology of devices (viz. Callon, Millo, and Muniesa 2007). If we are to seriously consider the complex process without the contingent, emergent, and unpredictable associational logics of certain assemblages, this process must involve something of a habitus, disposition, ethic, or spirit that infuses some associational forms and precipitates into actual, existing crystallizations of the social. This is exactly how I see the spirit of the "bear" entering into the devices (instruments) of the financial market. Absent such a proposal, the world of the device, so brilliantly portrayed by Callon and his colleagues and interlocutors, appears to be a self-animating device, a static crystallization of the precise sort that Latour urges us not to assume as constituting the social a priori. In proposing that my argument about a Weberian approach to the spirit of capitalism might motivate the crystallization of the Latourian device to animate the Callonian device, I am, in one sense, doing no more than to recover an idea that first occurred to me (albeit in a highly primitive form) when I wrote the introduction to *The Social Life of Things* (1986).

CHAPTER FOUR

THE SACRED MARKET

The Anthropology of Objects

Since finance today involves objects whose materiality seems both real and unreal, it seems appropriate to begin this chapter about the sacredness of the market with a quick review of the anthropology of objects, things, and material culture in general. The field has its dual origins in Marx and Mauss, and has been a venerable source of inspiration for anthropologists, who return, ever renewed, to the classic works of Malinowski on the kula (1922), Evans-Pritchard on cattle (1940), Boas on the potlatch (1921), and the like. A later generation of giants explored other contexts in these traditions of inquiry: they included Clifford Geertz's path-breaking work on the Moroccan bazaar (1978), Annette Weiner on Trobriand textiles (1991), Sahlins on Stone Age economics (1972), and Bourdieu on the tactics of gift-giving among the Kabyle (1976). Today, our active senior generation pursues such complex materialities as those of aboriginal art (Myers 2002), the human genome (Pálsson and Rabinow 1999), embryos and fetuses (Ginsburg and Rapp 1995), and other harder-to-identify flying objects. Archaeologists, who have always relied on the material record, continue to do inventive work on the place of tools, habitations, animal and human remains, and on those traces of our long history as a species that are left in art, jewelry, bone, iron, and cloth. And our newest generation has begun to study the most challenging features of our global economy by examining Chicago trading floors (Zaloom 2006), Japanese stockbrokers (Miyazaki 2013), Islamic bankers (Maurer 2005), and other tools and actors in the space of global finance. Here they join debates with the vigorous field of sociological studies of objects, inaugurated by Michel Callon and Bruno Latour. In this chapter I return to Emile Durkheim and ask how he might guide us in the anthropological study of today's economy and help us to develop a cultural view of the current epoch of intense financialization.

The Market

I begin by noting the enormous and still-undertheorized role of the market as a cultural fact in our world today in the United States. A venerable line of anthropologists, from Karl Polanyi to Marshall Sahlins, has alerted us to the status of the market as a central feature of the bourgeois social imaginary. Likewise, fine scholars such as Keith Hart (2000) and Timothy Mitchell (1998) have alerted us to the specific and historically constituted features of such abstractions as the economy and the market through the disciplines of economics and modern social theory. And yet its role in our lives remains underestimated.

Today, the market is a massive Durkheimian social fact. In his classic study of *The Elementary Forms of the Religious Life* (1995), Durkheim attempted to ground Kant's ideas about the source of the categorical imperative in his brilliant rereading of Spencer and Gillen's pathbreaking ethnographies of aboriginal Australia. His primary argument was breathtaking in its simplicity. He said that what these aborigines experienced, celebrated, and symbolized as sacred was none other than the externalized force of society in their inner moral lives. In other words, those things that each aboriginal self experienced as moral, regulative, awesome, binding, and meaningful in their persons was externalized and hypostasized as the sacred. This insight was generalized by Durkheim as an explanation of the presence of some idea of a transcendent divinity in all human societies. This argument remains the most radical secularizing argument of modern times, more even than those of Marx, Nietzsche, and Freud, all great demystifiers of the sacred.

Durkheim went on to reread a series of specific practices, beliefs, and symbols in the ethnographies of Spencer and Gillen to show that they were all evidence for his argument about aboriginal totemism, aboriginal rituals, and aboriginal religious objects (such as the famous *churinga*). This is not the place to discuss the numerous subsequent debates about Durkheim's readings or misreadings of the ethnographies of Australia available to him, or to dwell on the massive debt of many major anthropologists since then to him, a list that includes Lévi-Strauss, Bourdieu, and Sahlins, to name only three.

We could perform a parallel operation on the market today, with the only required adjustment being to replace the idea of society with that of the market. That is, our sacred world is largely nothing other than the reality of our social selves externalized into the abstraction of the market. Thus, to be precise, since the sacred as such (in its explicit, organized religious forms) is a niche demographic in our own society, the real mystification is the externalization of the social onto the image not of society but of the market. Thus the market acquires the authority and logical priority of something within us that we experience as the transcendent, moral, and ethical source of order in our lives. This happens not, of course, by some single flash of conversion or conviction but through the steady reproductive force of a host of practices, beliefs, rituals, and symbols, embedded in a cosmology that lends ongoing conviction to something that is real but not wholly open to conscious examination, something exactly like society for Durkheim. If Durkheim were to have conducted an ethnographic inquiry into the contemporary United States, he would have had to conclude that the sacred was nothing other than the market, duly externalized. For this argument to hold, the devil is in the details, so we must examine at least some of our everyday practices and convictions in order to test this claim. I do so by looking not at the market as a whole but at that aspect of it that is captured by the term "financialization."

One caution is immediately in order. I am not just suggesting that we are dominated more than ever before by large economic interests, though that is true. Nor am I simply echoing the well-developed Marxist insight that bourgeois thought is an ideological reflex of modern capitalism, though that too may be true. Nor am I simply bemoaning the greed, materialism, and wealth-obsession of many Americans today, though that too is a legitimate observation. Nor am I simply complaining about the Wall Street's cynical contempt for Main Street, though that view is also evident. I am after something more foundational, more elusive, and more consequential.

Financial Materiality

A simple cross-cultural definition of religion could be that it is that set of meanings and practices through which we render the invisible world visible and tractable to human interests. As ideas of what is invisible are culturally varied, so are those religions to which they give rise. A large part of what we today engage in our efforts to make the invisible world both visible and manageable is the financial side of our lives as market beings. Let me look at a few basic forms of this mediation. Let us start with plastic. The cards almost all of us carry in our wallets or handbags usually include a credit or debit card, an ATM card, and one or more shopping cards for particular stores. Many of us carry many more. These plastic objects are our lifelines. We do not usually know the fine print associated with most of them, but we take them seriously for they are often the key to 95 percent of our material lives. We would die without them. Let me show you a bit of the significance of plastic in the United States today:

Consider just one number: Total US revolving debt (98% of which is made up of credit card debt): $793.1 billion, as of May 2011 (Simon 2011)

This stunning number ($793.1 billion) should give us pause. It measures one dimension of my Durkheimian view of the market as a collective social fact in the United States today. The US GNP is now about $14 trillion. That is, one out of every two thousand US dollars is in some form of circulating consumer debt. The proportion might seem small. But let us try another number. Look at the total US consumer debt number, as opposed to the revolving debt: it is $2.43 trillion, which is about 15 percent of the US GNP. Consider one final number, the Household Debt Service Ratio, which is the ratio of our debt service payments to our disposable personal incomes: for renters it is about 25 percent and for mortgage holders it is about 15 percent.

What do these numbers mean from our neo-Durkheimian point of view? If we pick the mid-point between debt service payments for renters and for home mortgage holders, and place it at 20 percent, one-fifth of what we householders earn is spent on and for plastic of one or another sort. I am not here directly concerned with the political economy of this state of affairs, of the horrendous implications of being a debt-driven economy, or of the links of this fact to the current employment statistics and the recession as a whole. Rather, I want to point out that the world of plastic is tied to our routine means of reproduction on an everyday basis, that the larger implications of our collective predicament are largely unknown and unseen by us, that the means of this form of reproduction are problematically magical and above all, that these precarious forms of debt-driven daily life are largely now commonsense to the American consumer. The mechanisms for this naturalization are addressed later in this chapter.

Or consider stocks and the stock market. We have largely forgotten what a strange and abstract form of collective valuation is congealed and mystified in our current stock market. Stocks in companies are a peculiar form of wealth, whose value is measured by such unreliable indicators as price-to-earnings ratios. In reality stock prices are largely self-fulfilling phenomena of the stock market itself. The stock market is not a market for items that actually have their value in some other sphere but is in fact the source of the value of stocks, itself constantly volatile due to the actions of stock buyers, sellers, traders, brokers, and others, based on criteria that are themselves intrinsically opaque. The value of stocks, and concepts such as "undervaluation," which is the lifelong principle of "value" investors like Warren Buffet, is itself quite mysterious, for a number of reasons but mostly because stocks measure a metavalue, or, if you wish, the price of a value which is itself an abstraction. This would not matter if a large number of Americans were not directly tied to the stock market, either as pension holders, small investors, day-traders, or employees of companies whose policies are driven by stock market valuations, and by a number of other market-based speculative organizations (such as hedge funds) that regularly influence stock prices through their own actions or nonactions.

From a Durkheimian perspective, the stock market could be seen as a vast array of totemic groupings, arranged in different sets, classifications, and series such as growth stocks, tech stocks, emerging market stocks, and the like, each of which is allied to different beliefs and cults associated with their strengths and weaknesses. This argument about stocks can also be extended to other instruments such as bonds, though the relative limited access of ordinary investors to the sale and of purchase of bonds makes them of more specialized interest. In sheer quantitative terms, however, bonds represent a vastly huger market than stocks. This totemic analogy is not frivolous. Named categories of stocks eventually become granulated into the names, that is, listed names, of specific companies, each of which is presided over for the purposes of the stock market by different categories of analysts and brokers who specialize in specific industries. The endless serialization and classification of stocks is a matter to which I will return.

Or consider mortgages, specifically housing mortgages. The bizarreness of this form of mediated financial materiality has only risen to public attention because of the meltdown of 2008, in which new forms of bundled mortgage derivatives played a massive role in the market collapse, the effects of which are still very much with us. Even a simple housing mortgage is a mysterious thing. It is an instrument of home "ownership" in which the so-called homeowner owns only the mortgage but not the house, except at the end point of a long horizon of amortization, which is in its own right a somewhat mysterious mechanism. Meanwhile, the lending bank is the real owner, who, like a dying shark, only with its last breath gives up its deadly hold on the house. Meanwhile the cost of this peculiar form of co-ownership is borne by the mortgage owner in the form of interest, which is substantially the profit of the bank. The effort to evacuate the principal and front-load interest is what produced the most toxic categories of bad mortgage loans in US history over the last decade.

Amortization is in itself a mysterious mechanism with which to repay debts for loans over a long period (with variable amounts of principal and interest combining over time to repay the loan). That amortization has become part of the common sense of any homeowner in this country, is a testimony to the depth at which the abstracting logics of contemporary financial capitalism have become naturalized as common sense. Housing loans (mortgages) are an essential part of the material life of financial objects in the United States because they take a mythic element of the contemporary cosmology of capitalism, in which your "own" house is treated as the mark of financial adulthood and security, all housing values are always supposed to rise, and though what you own is a piece of paper, you are led to believe that you actually own a house. The bizarre materiality of the mortgage-backed American house is that while its visible material form is relatively fixed, bounded, and indivisible, its financial form, the mortgage, has now been structured to be endlessly divisible, recombinable, saleable, and leverage-able for financial speculators, in a manner that is both mysterious and toxic.

Consider another staple of the average American lifestyle or life-dream: the pension. The pension is a relatively legible form of social security, that in other societies is provided by family and kin who assure long-term hedges against old age, illness, and unexpected poverty. In the advanced industrial world, they have gradually become routinized elements of wage and salary arrangements, with considerable variation across corporate and private pension plans, with endless tax and benefit variations among them. The primary site where the visible and comprehensible benefits of pensions, especially in the United States, become tied to the invisible mysteries of the larger financial market is through the large-scale pension funds whose assets are themselves tied substantially to the stock market as well as to other instruments that carry various risk to return potentials. This is a graduated process of abstraction and mystification, in which the measurable and visible reality of a paycheck (with the pension withdrawal clearly stated) is the starting point of a journey to the financial stratosphere. Once again the visible meets the invisible through a series of steps of dematerialization.

Finally, the greatest single source of materialized mystification in the financial market place is the world of insurance, which also has its quotidian roots in the efforts of ordinary individuals to hedge against normal life risks such as sickness, job loss, and death, as well as to damage against property. The current insurance industry in the United States, which has the same roots as all modern insurance systems, in the historical interplay of statistical probability, overseas commerce, and gambling, today extends its tentacles into every nook and cranny of American life, from health and housing to life, to one's children's education, to natural hazards and to any imaginable life contingency. Furthermore, as we saw in the recent financial meltdown, the biggest insurance giant in the world, AIG, was the place where the buck stopped in terms of the long chain of derivative transactions enabled by toxic mortgage loans. Here, big insurance was not a hedge against risk for the common man. Rather, it was the guarantor of those who behaved most irresponsibly with other people's money. For our purposes, the interesting thing about the role of insurance in the financialization of everyday life, and the material mysteries of the cult of the market, is the transformation of risk itself into a speculative commodity as opposed to risk as something that opens up the possibility of profit through the gap between expectations and actual outcomes. Above all, insurance is the major site for the central technique of modern finance which is probabilistic calculation. I will return to this point in my conclusion.

Quality and Quantity

I have so far suggested that the market in the United States today is a space that replaces what for Durkheim was the space of society, creatively misrecognized as God or the sacred. I have noted how some of the basic means of the production of the everyday in our lives are products of the deep financialization of our world, which embed and naturalized complex means of abstraction and mediation between the spheres of the visible and the invisible in our apprehension of these worlds.

The means or instruments for producing the everyday are accompanied by a series of protocols that blur the relationship between quantity and quality, thus further strengthening their capacity to combine power with opacity in the reproduction of our identities. Principal among these are scores, ranks, ratings, and profiles. The FICO score is perhaps the most revolutionary of these scoring protocols and has been analyzed historically and analytically by Martha Poon (2008):

> The FICO credit bureau score, a commercially available consumer risk assessment tool, was originally one among many such metrics; the three companies that market credit scores under the brands of Trans Union, Equifax, and Experian initially offered competing metrics. In 1995, however, Freddie Mac decided to adopt FICO in order to standardize underwriting practices in federally sanctioned lending. FICO was then adopted by other lenders and rating agencies (including not only the three companies I just listed, but also Standard and Poor's, the equity rating agency), and by 2003 it had become the industry standard—in part because it could easily be operationalized through proprietary, automated underwriting software (Loan Prospector). With the adoption of FICO, credit-by-screening, or the case-by-case evaluation of potential borrowers as individuals, was replaced by credit-by-risk, an automated, quantitative assessment of risk pools that did not even require individual interviews. Once in place, the

score scale FICO created not only discriminated between a group of loans designated "prime" and those designated "subprime"; it also made it possible for loan originators to devise products for which members of the second group could qualify.

There are, of course, other scoring tools in wide use in American society for a variety of purposes, ranging from security alerts to SAT examinations to various insurance protocols for defining risk properties to pools of customers. What I especially wish to notice is that these scoring devices and protocols have the effect of permitting individuals to be profiled, grouped, and categorized for a variety of financial purposes, including those of making housing mortgage loans, a particular use whose toxic potentials were made clear in the housing meltdown of 2008. The relevance of these scoring protocols to my current argument is that they allow the qualities of individual lives (loans, family crises, housing purchases, health crises) to be converted into aggregate forms, which then allow a unique number to be assigned to any particular individual. These scores are used by all major credit-rating agencies. The transformation of a unique life project into a unique risk score is a remarkable operation that quantifies quality and renders it pseudo-qualitative by its role as an individual marker. This reindividualization is a critical move that guarantees the capacity of the larger system to engage individuals and households in a manner that goes beyond the profile to the personalized score.

Scores such as the FICO score take their force from the general proliferation of scoring, rating, ranking, and profiling in all advanced industrial economies and especially in the contemporary United States. They constitute the assemblage of technical means by which the relationship between quantity and quality is blurred and this blurring in turn facilitates the special traffic between the visible and invisible structures of the heavily financialized market.

In general these tools follow the following sequence: First, the initial conversion of select events, desires, or actions by the consumer into some sort of numerical equivalent; second, the aggregation of these numbers into some sort of aggregate profile; third, the reshaping of this profile into various categories and groups relevant to the interests of the manager, trader, speculator, or insurer; fourth, the reconversion of the individual as a translated subject into the object of specific actions, communications, and decisions (such as a negative or positive loan request, a positive or negative credit card application, a positive or negative college or insurance application, or varying and personalized degrees of attention from debt collectors, investment counselors, colleges, banks, and the like). At the same time these scores, ranking, ratings, and profiles are the basis of a large variety of transactions invisible to the individual consumer, notably those that involve slicing and dicing these profiles into numerous forms of speculative profit-making. This feature of infinite divisibility and recombinability is at the very heart of the reconstitution of the modern financial subject.

Narratives and Social Forms

The production of this sort of financial subject could not occur without a rich stock of narratives, scripts, and stories that give cosmological heft to its instruments. And there is no dearth of such narratives. Here we need to recognize that we have all been turned into business junkies through the mass media in the last three decades or so.

Business news was a specialized affair in the late 1960s, confined to a few magazines such as *Money* and *Fortune*, and to a newspapers and TV reporters (not channels). Now, it is hard to find anything but business as the topic of news in all media. Consider television: if you spend even three hours surfing between CNN and BBC on any given day (surfing for news about Libya or about soccer, for example) you will find yourself regularly assaulted by business news, not just from London, New York, and Washington, but from Singapore, Hong Kong, Mumbai, and many other places. Look at the serious talk shows and chances are that you will find a talking CEO, describing what's good about his company, what's bad about the government, and how to read his company's stock prices. Channels like MSNBC are a form of endless, mind-numbing Jerry Lewis telethon about the economy, with more than a hint of the desperation of the Depression movie *They Shoot Horses, Don't They?* (1969), as they bid the viewer to make insane bets and to mourn the fallen heroes of failed companies and fired CEOs.

Turn to the newspapers and things get worse. Any reader of the *New York Times* will find it hard to get away from the business machine. Start with the lead section, and stories about Obama's economic plans, strange Republican proposals about taxes, the Euro-crisis, and the latest bank scandal will assault you. Some relief is provided by more corporate news: the exit (and now the death) of Steve Jobs, the op-ed piece about the responsibilities of the super-rich by Warren Buffet, Donald Trump advertising his new line of housewares to go along with his unattractive homes and buildings. Turn to the sports section: it is littered with talk of franchises, salaries, trades, owner antics, stadium projects, and more. I need hardly say anything about the section on "Business" itself, which has now virtually become redundant. And if you are still thirsty for more business news, check out the "Home," "Lifestyle," and "Real Estate" sections for news on houses you can't afford and mortgage financing gimmicks you have never heard off. Some measure of relief is to be in the occasional "Science Times" and in the *New York Times Book Review*, which do have some pieces that are not primarily about profit, corporate politics or the recession.

The *New York Times* alone is not to blame for this. They are the newspaper of "record" and that means that they reflect broader trends and cannot be blamed for their compliance with bigger trends. Go through the magazines when you take a flight to Detroit or Mumbai and there is again a feast of news geared to the "business traveler." This is when I catch up on how to negotiate the best deal, why this is the time to buy gold, and what software and hardware to use when I make my next presentation to General Electric. These examples could be multiplied in any number of bookstores, newspaper kiosks, airport lounges, park benches, and dentists' offices.

This avalanche of business news is the main mechanism through which we have been resubjectified by the business world and turned into compliant financial subjects. And it is accompanied by all the requirements of any persuasive cosmology: it has its heroes and demons, its paradigmatic characters and situations, its key stories of financial chicanery, heroism, rise and fall. It is a full-fledged cosmology, able to account for great achievements and spectacular failures, as well as the virtues of being good members of what I earlier referred to as the faith-based economy, one in which we are persuaded to shop, borrow, toil, and strive even as our mortgages are foreclosed, our credit cards canceled, our loan applications denied, and our jobs pink-slipped.

And this cosmology has produced its deep array of dominant social forms: the corporation, the class action suit, the employer pension collectives, the investor clubs, the chambers of commerce, and the like, which constitute our real social structure beneath the apparent persistence of friends, family, and neighbors. These social forms, which also crystallize themselves on trading floors, financial back offices, regulatory agencies, financial media networks, and other mediating social entities, deserve careful study in their own right, as they have now begun to receive.

Probability and Personhood

I return now to the implications of a Durkheimian approach to the era of financialization. In fact, regarding modern life, Durkheim was deeply influenced by Schopenhauer and oscillated between optimism and pessimism in his own writings and reflections. I now offer a pessimistic twist to the Durkheimian analysis of financialization that I have offered.

The enchantment of the market, its dramatic success in replacing society as the site of the sacred in human life, poses deep problems that we have understood at least since the time of Marx. In light of the

Durkheimian perspective that I have proposed on the financialized epoch of capitalism in which we live, there is a further reason for critical anxiety. Durkheim and his closest followers, including Marcel Mauss, were above all concerned with the category of the person, a tradition of interest that remains alive and vital in anthropology today.

The techniques, devices, and practices of contemporary finance produce a certain form of subjectivity by a process of endless division, granulation, slicing and dicing of the person, which then allows the reassemblage of persons as subjects, through the visible means of credit scores, debt, mortgage, stocks, and so on, all of which depend on an initial atomization of the person according to the abstractions of finance. All these techniques rely on the empire of probability, on the production of statistical protocols of risk, profit, and calculated expectations. Probability is the underlying epistemology of contemporary finance, cutting across insurance, stocks, credit, mortgages, and much else in the financial world.

The epistemology of probability has the effect of producing radical discontinuity between the atomized elements of the person, which are distributed across various aggregated temporal maps, and protocols of risk. This atomization recalls the central question posed by the British philosopher Derek Parfit (1984), who has criticized all utilitarian approaches to ethics by showing that such approaches see the relationships between different persons at any single point in time but do not address the problem that each of us is, in an important sense, a different person at different points over time.

In the world of contemporary finance, this discontinuity between our atomized selves over time is not seen as a profound ethical problem. Rather it is treated as a massive opportunity for reassembling these divided bits of the person into various forms of financial subject tractable to the making of financial profit. Thus we have a discontinuous ethical subject, a fragmented Durkheimian person, without any identifiable moral mechanism for reaggregation or social cohesion.

Thus the replacement of society by the market, in my argument, certainly supports a Durkheimian analysis of its success as a cosmology for connecting the invisible to the visible forces in our worlds but it also pulls the rug out from any sort of Durkheimian hope for connectivity, solidarity, and moral community. The challenge both for anthropology and for us as citizens is how to make this observation the foundation for new forms of critique and resistance.

CHAPTER FIVE

SOCIALITY, UNCERTAINTY, AND RITUAL

A possible dialogue between Weber and Durkheim, as I have already implied, has been an inert and unexploited part of the legacy of the social sciences. Along with Marx, they are frequently seen as forming the triumvirate of founders of the modern social sciences. The dialogue between Weber and Marx was rich and lively in Weber's own work, and in scholars working in the Weberian tradition ever since. The dialogue between Durkheim and Marx has been more muted but, especially in the hands of Marcel Mauss and his followers in anthropology, the presence of Marx is never minor. Weber and Durkheim, who lived essentially through the same decades of the late nineteenth and early twentieth centuries, had no direct exchanges and this absence is itself a subject of much speculation among historians of sociology. This curious nondialogue has been reified by the separate histories of sociology and anthropology in the United States and in Europe, where Durkheim became the canonic founder of anthropology and Weber his counterpart for sociology. They are frequently in each other's company in textbooks and anthologies, but rarely in breakthrough work in either discipline. Bourdieu may be considered the closest recent thinker to have benefited equally from Durkheim and Weber, though in idiosyncratic ways.

Weber's famous thesis on the role of the Protestant ethic in relation to the unique event of modern occidental capitalism, discussed already in various parts of this book, is saturated by his ideas about uncertainty and is virtually innocent of any serious interest in risk. In this sense,

Frank Knight, who was greatly influenced by Weber, is rightly seen as the source of all our serious current ideas about risk and uncertainty, with others like Schumpeter serving as ancillary thinkers concerned with entrepreneurship and innovation.

Uncertainty in Weber's account of the Protestant ethic was primarily existential or salvational. It had little to do with the primary conditions of early capitalism. The connection was historically derived, secondary, and gradual in its emergence. In a word, uncertainty about whether a member of the Puritan middle classes was or was not one of the elect (the saved) was the paramount uncertainty for precapitalist Puritans, especially the Calvinists. Being a product of God's grace, and being determined in advance by the mystery of divine predestination, salvation was completely indifferent to human knowledge, effort, or manipulation. Further, it could not be read as a precondition of any human accomplishment or good fortune, such as wealth, power, or respectability in this world. It was both unknown and unknowable.

Weber's effort to account for the links between the specifically occidental form of entrepreneurial capitalism, begun in 1904–5, with the publication of his classic essay on *The Protestant Ethic and the Spirit of Capitalism* (2009) was not really completed until the last years of his life, toward the end of the First World War, when he gave a magisterial series of lectures on the comparative ethics, ethos, and social force of the great world religions. In between lay a lifetime of explorations of Roman law and agrarian life (the topic of his first extended scholarly work in *Roman Agrarian History* [2008]), of the journey of commercial enterprises from the Roman period until the mature capitalism of his own lifetime, of law, economy, and the city in the West and in India, China, and the Islamic world, and of much else besides.

Weber's main observations about the relationship between Puritanism and the ethos of occidental capitalism did not change dramatically through these decades. He found its anchor in the peculiar salvational uncertainty of Calvinism, which was engaged by a small group of European merchants in the form of an effort to systematize and rationalize their individual lives through the rigorous practice of capitalist profit-making, not simply to make a profit, but rather to organize their lives as a kind of experiment in rational management. Thus double-entry bookkeeping was a critical element of Weber's understanding of the transition from feudal forms of commerce and profit-seeking to the sober, judicious, methodical (all Weberian terms) making of profit by the rational methods of the modern manufacturing enterprise. This rational disposition was deeply antithetical to the adventurous, speculative, and hedonistic spirit of all prior forms in which wealth had been pursued.

Systematic profit-making was a byproduct of this lifestyle, whose main aim was to offer the sober asceticism of the Puritan businessman as a celebration of God's grace, which could also be a *possible* sign of election by that very divine grace. The application of the techniques of double-entry bookkeeping to the practices of capitalist manufacturing was a way to bring one's life under a single and systematic regimen of discipline, in which thrift, sobriety, and discipline were the cardinal virtues. They constituted parts of an aspirational form of religious performance that could index a life that God had already chosen to be that of one who had been saved. This disposition was enacted by making one's entire life a wager on the possibility that one was in fact one of the elect, even though there could be no possible certainty about this fact. Notice that financial risk, or any form of probabilistic calculation, was no part of Weber's picture of the ethical life of the Puritan entrepreneur. One might say that this Puritan type operated entirely on the principle of risk-free profit, if by profit was meant the possibility of having merited God's grace. Profit in the world of the economy was merely a method of allaying uncertainty.

The Puritan entrepreneurial life, in this Weberian account, may indeed be seen as one massive life-long ritual performance, but it was a performance that always involved a *coproductive and mutually catalytic relationship between certainty and uncertainty*. Certainty was produced by the practice of methodical profit-making but continuing uncertainty was an existential condition that could not be resolved in this life, whatever one's ethical efforts. A life of this type was a continuing effort to reset the relationship between certainty and uncertainty, with profit-making in business as a constant effort and salvational uncertainty as a background reality, given by the theological model.

When we turn to Durkheim, the picture is somewhat different. Durkheim was also concerned with understanding what Weber would have called the disenchantment of modern life, the cost that was paid in terms of anomie, uncertainty, and impersonality in the course of the transition from *Gemeinschaft* to *Gesellschaft*. Like Weber, Durkheim explored this transition in many domains, including religion, politics, labor, and education. Also like Weber, Durkheim saw sociology as a moral vocation whose task was to offer a window into the moral life of modern society, and indeed to understand social life itself, a primary mystery and puzzle. This led Durkheim (and his later followers, most importantly Marcel Mauss) to ponder what held human societies together, what moral force pulled individuals together, and what made them conform to social norms and institutional rules, especially when the bonds of the social had begun to be eroded by the ravages of capitalist economic organizations and forms. Unlike Weber, whose sociology remained anchored in the meaning-making proclivities of the individual, Durkheim gradually came to see society as a moral force that could not be understood simply as the product of willful contract between well-formed, already social creatures. For Durkheim, society had its own force—crystallized in what he called collective representations and the "collective conscience"—and was a primary and primordial source of all that was properly human. Man was thus an irreducibly social creature, even if he did not always recognize this in his everyday life. This view of man's irreducibly social nature was the underlying theme of all of Durkheim's major works, on the sociological method, on suicide, on education, on the division of labor, and above all on religion.

But there are two reasons why we cannot simply apply Durkheim's ideas to contemporary finance, and in fact need to extend or reinvent his

line of thought. The first is that we need to move beyond his functionalist tendencies, which simply see ritual as a solution to an external problem posed by social life, which is its transitory, entropic, and amoral
nature. The second is that we need to concede that Durkheim would
have been startled by the foundational place of risk and uncertainty as
fundamental properties of market society in contemporary times, beyond the dynamics of exchange, calculation, and commodification. To
tackle the first problem, we need to reconsider the standard model of
ritual in social life, which is at least as old as Durkheim.

To address this problem, we need to briefly recall that part of the
history of anthropology has always been characterized by an interest
in ritual action, logic, and mentality. Though numerous major strands
of thinking have been associated with the giants of early anthropology
(Durkheim, van Gennep, Malinowski, Evans-Pritchard, among others), there is remarkable consistency in seeing ritual (sometimes seen
as equivalent to magic) as part of a near-universal apparatus for hedging
against danger, uncertainty, and randomness in social life. This "hedging" view of ritual, which is part of a deep tradition of thinking about
magic as a form of technology, begins in a functionalist effort to see
ritual as "doing" something important in social life. It lives on today in
most colloquial uses of the word "ritual," which overwhelmingly em-
phasize its capacity to produce routine, regularity, and predictability in
social life, through practices of etiquette, personal routine, or collective
discipline.

The major deviation from this functionalist perspective within anthropology is connected to the effort to bring Austinian ideas of "performativity" into the study of ritual, associated primarily with Tambiah
(1985), and a few other linguistically inclined cultural anthropologists
more recently (LiPuma and Lee 2004). The general accomplishment
of this line of work, based on the important work of the philosopher
J. L. Austin, was to shift our understanding of the work of ritual away
from the plane of science and technology to the plane of language, and in
particular to the place of "performatives," that is, that class of speech acts

that achieves effects in the state of the world through their proper utterance in context. The idea that words could "do" things rather than just "mean" things revealed that the linguistic dimensions of ritual (which provide the main semantic map of the ritual) could be regarded as performative forms that changed the world by the force (illocutionary and perlocutionary) of their utterance. While there has been much technical debate about (and refinement of) this approach, it remains the single most important theoretical development in the study of ritual in the twentieth century.

The next major step in this line of thinking is most clearly associated with Judith Butler (1990, 1997, 2004), who, in a series of works applying speech act theory to literary works as well as to new movements in sexual and gender politics, saw that speech acts could also be deployed in such a manner as to alter the conditions of felicity that they appeared to presuppose. This development in the cultural understanding of the role of performatives in social life has yet to be worked out and has not been fully absorbed by anthropological students of ritual, until some recent efforts to analyze what might be called retro-performativity in ritual and in social life.

The retro-performativity argument is a fundamentally new angle on the relationship between performatives and their conditions of felicity, in which certain performatives are seen to create, through their agency and effect, the very conditions of felicity that they also causally presuppose. In the case of ritual performances, what this would mean is that a particular sequence of words and actions in a given ritual setting is actually part of a claim, which, if effective, retrospectively implies the existence of a set of felicitous preconditions. Thus, in a ritual of pig-exchange between exchanging groups of affines, the success of a negotiated gift of pigs between one party and another would actually produce the effect of designating the two groups as appropriate affines, something that the exchange actually presupposed. This retro-creativity of certain performatives introduces a radical new element into our understanding of the performativity of rituals, since it exposes the fact that the entire ritual is an exercise in *enacting uncertainty in such a form as to increase the likelihood of resolving it.*

Let us examine this approach more closely. We can begin by supposing that all rituals have this retro-performative element, even if to different degrees. Whenever two parties enter into a ritual transaction, they are, in the first instance, staging or enacting a radical uncertainty. In what does the uncertainty consist? First, the uncertainty consists in the unknown question of whether there will be a counterparty to the proposed transaction *at all*: take the simple case of the extended hand that is not met by another, creating the unfulfilled handshake and the awkward dangling hand of the offerer. The second risk is that there will be a counterparty and so the ritual will proceed but something about what is put on the table is found either excessive or lacking (too many pigs or too few) *after the ritual is concluded*, thus making the ritual, at least to some extent, a failure. The final risk is that there will be some unforeseen technical failure of materials, method, or expertise, or an "act of God" (such as the death of an important kinsperson at the very same moment as a marriage ritual) that renders the ritual null and void (or even inauspicious). Each of these uncertainties has to be successfully avoided in order for the ritual to have its retrospective effect in creating the desired relationship, by ratifying the very relationships that the ritual presupposes.

How much can we generalize this view of ritual, regarded as a framework *for the co-staging of uncertainty and certainty*? While it would require a thorough examination of the archive of anthropology to provide a strong answer to this question, there is merit to the hypothesis that this co-staging, which is always premised on some degree of retro-performativity, is endemic to all ritual processes, such as the classic rituals of birth, death, the agrarian calendar, and prosperity, the management of encounters with guests and kinsmen, and the consecration of new spaces, dwellings, and territories. One test of this hypothesis (which we can only signal in the context of this chapter) would be found in a re-examination of the classic work by Arnold van Gennep on

The Rites of Passage (1960) and at three important modern extensions of the van Gennep argument (Appadurai 2013; Girard 1977; Turner 1967) in regard to rituals with a sacrificial element in which a person, or a part of a person, is sacrificed in the interest of reproducing some sort of social and cosmological whole.

The second challenge that faces anyone who wishes to employ a Durkheimian strategy in relation to the contemporary world of finance, which is that Durkheim had no understanding of the looming place of risk and uncertainty in the workings of the market, especially in its most recent, financialized phase. Does this disqualify Durkheim's value for our purposes? I think not, and here is why.

The Australian Aboriginals whose ritual practices were (as reported by earlier ethnographers) the primary descriptive basis for Durkheim's arguments in *The Elementary Forms of the Religious Life* (1995) can also be seen as addressing a fundamental uncertainty (just as Weber's Puritans were dealing with the fundamental uncertainty of salvation). Their uncertainty was the uncertainty about the existence of a larger social collectivity as such, given the material conditions of their ordinary lives, which were spent as small and scattered groups, which met as larger groups only occasionally, across vast distances and against many challenges of material and social entropy. For them, a larger social reality was itself uncertain, hard won, and periodic. Their uncertainty was whether or not there was something larger than themselves, some form of social and collective being that was more credible, more celebratory, more euphoric, more reflexive, and more enduring than the small bands in which they conducted most of their quotidian social lives, wandering in the harsh conditions of the Australian outback. The significance of their periodic large-scale ritual celebrations (reported by Spencer and Gillen and reinterpreted by Durkheim) was the *rediscovery of the social as such*. This is what accounts for the ecstatic, celebratory, and the magical in these great ritual encounters, and accounts for Durkheim's use of the evocative phrase "collective effervescence," which he used to capture the ethos of these major events. Durkheim did not quite formulate the problem of the social this way, but it is an entirely Durkheimian observation. The foundational uncertainty of Australian aboriginal life is whether there is a larger social whole to which the small roving bands that eked out a difficult life for weeks and months actually belonged, which was more reliable, more joyous, and more permanent. The ritual performances that Durkheim analyzed are indeed an elaborate restaging, simultaneously, both of this uncertainty and the certainty that such a larger social order exists.

How then do Weber and Durkheim illuminate one another, if this reading of ritual as a co-staging of certainty and uncertainty in social life is correct? To answer this question requires us to distance ourselves from the routinized adjacency of Weber and Durkheim (in most canonic accounts) and to re-examine the ways in which each of them moves us away from the standard reading of ritual as a standard and universal human way of *reducing* uncertainty in social life. This view is based on the metaphorical force of ritual, its reduced picture of what really counts in the world, and its simple and repetitive patterns, which lend themselves to easy standardization, replication, and re-enactment. This view, which I earlier characterized as functionalist, might be called the "standard" view of ritual and is the main way in which ritual is commonly understood both in the social sciences and in most colloquial usages. We need a more nuanced view in order to make the journey back from Weber and Durkheim to Marx and forward from Weber and Durkheim to the world of the financial derivative.

Recall the earlier reading of Weber. We can now say that what Weber's Puritan merchants may be seen to have been doing, just as Durkheim's Australian Aboriginals may be regarded as doing, is to retro-engineer the foundational assumption of their respective worlds through the procedures of their rituals. That is, they co-stage the foundational uncertainty of their cosmologies and its possible transformation, even though it is temporary, into some form of certainty. In the Puritan case, the foundational uncertainty is about whether the actor is one of the saved. He engages this uncertainty by its ritual enactment in the space of profit-making and through the production of profit, he creates the sign of profit through methodicality, across his entire life, thus resolving this uncertainty, though in a manner that can never be settled once and for all. The Australian Aboriginal does something similar with his foundational uncertainty, which is whether there is a larger social collectivity at all, apart from his grim and transient quotidian life as a member of a small, nomadic group. The Australian rituals performed periodically (such as the famous corroboree) restage both the question and the answer in a powerful but temporary manner, which works for some time, but requires regular restaging and repetition, without cease, for the sensation of sociality to be sustained over the long run.

In short, both Weber and Durkheim offer us routes for understanding how the foundational uncertainties of any particular social group require ritual performance that, through the mechanism of retro-performativity, allows the *temporary* achievement of certainty by staging them *within the same ritual context, idiom and constraints*. This rereading of Weber and Durkheim, which opens up a new way to explore their mutual productivity, also allows us to look further back, to ask what Marx might have missed from this point of view, and also to look forward to the world of financial action inspired by Black-Scholes.[1]

I have argued that Weber and Durkheim offer us an understanding of the co-presence of uncertainty and certainty in ritualized social orders (e.g., religious, magical). The central problem of financial practice in the domain of derivatives is the problem of arriving at options pricing in real-time trades, given that the available models for options pricing (especially Black-Scholes and all its elaborations) do not offer unambiguous predictions about options prices. Several recent commentators (Ayache 2010; Derman 2011; MacKenzie 2006) seem to be struggling for a language to describe the ways in which the "social" enters into trading decisions when the models provide no decisive guidance. I have suggested in this chapter that a rereading of Weber and Durkheim from the point of view of this gap in current theories of derivatives trading offers a richer and fuller way of grasping how the social enters into trading practice. The joint deployment of some ideas of Weber and Durkheim on what we might call ritual practice "under conditions of uncertainty" can provide a bridge into how traders make the leap from the space of probability (quantifiable) to the space of uncertainty (unquantifiable).

The relationship of cosmology (the model) to ritual (the actual activity of trading) is not symmetrical. Ritual practice is an effort to recalibrate the world (as it exists) so as to achieve a closer relationship to the cosmos (ideally a relationship of identity); financial practice is an effort to use the model to recalibrate the actually existing world so as to generate riskless return. This relationship of symmetry and inversion between the worlds of ritual and of trading comes into play because of the role of the *interval* (timing and duration between the present and any specific future date) and the peculiar nature of retro-performativity in the ritual and financial spheres.

Both ritual practitioners and traders are aware of the constant slippage between their models and prices or values in the world as it exists. The value of looking at how Weber and Durkheim see ritual for understanding the world of traders is that it offers a robust account of what traders actually do with the gap between probability and uncertainty in the world of derivatives. The contrarian trader (the short seller) may be regarded as someone who both relies on and opposes the wisdom of the crowd. He exploits the ambiguity of Weber's charisma and of Durkheim's collective effervescence, both of which are group phenomena and appear to foreclose the contrarian. Yet because the contrarian also exploits the moment of contingency, the wave of collective effervescence, he belongs to his wider social environment, which cannot be understood without a closer look at the charismatic nature of the derivative, which produces a force that both contrarians and more conventional traders must inhabit and negotiate.

CHAPTER SIX

THE CHARISMATIC
DERIVATIVE

A *derivative* is a financial instrument whose value is based on one or more underlying assets. In practice, it is a contract between two parties that specifies conditions (especially the dates, resulting values of the underlying variables, and notional amounts) under which payments are to be made between the parties. The most common types of derivatives are: forwards, futures, options, and swaps. The most common underlying assets include: commodities, stocks, bonds, interest rates, and currencies.

Wikipedia

The challenge of understanding financial derivatives can be addressed by returning to some important ideas of Emile Durkheim and Max Weber. In this chapter, I suggest a way in which some ideas of Durkheim and Weber, which have largely led to different habits and styles of social inquiry, can more fruitfully be reconnected to one another. If my proposal is viable, it also offers a positive reading of the potential of the derivative form to be a tool of financial inclusion and wealth generation, rather than of increased speculation, exploitation, and immiseration. It also opens up some new readings of Durkheim and Weber.

My understanding of financial derivatives is in particular owed to LiPuma and Lee (2004), MacKenzie (2006), Martin (2007, 2011), and Ayache (2010). I am especially convinced by Ayache's claim that derivatives constitute a sort of *contingent claim by market-makers engaged in creating prices through trading.*

Ayache's 2010 book *The Blank Swan* is already the subject of considerable controversy, and has even been criticized as some sort of spoof or satire. More moderate critics complain about its dense French philosophical prose, its repetitious, often hermetic writing style, and its aphoristic assertions. What I take from Ayache is not so much the reliability of his arguments or even the accuracy of his characterizations of financial instruments and processes. Rather, I find productive his effort to open up for scrutiny the habitus of contemporary financial thinking, and to expose the structure of its underling doxa about probability, price, market, and value, among other fundamentals of the financial world.

Ayache's major claim, to my mind, is that the fact that prices are expressed in numbers has led to the mistaken belief that these numbers belong to temporal sets that are susceptible to probabilistic understanding. Ayache's entire argument about contingency, price, trading, and markets is based on the refutation of this massive consensus and leads him to propose that we need to make a radical distinction between probability (including ideas about outliers, random walks, and fat tails) and simply consider prices, particularly those that the market provides or admits for derivatives, as being radical contingent events that are created without reference to any preceding patterns, trends, tendencies, or causes. They are generated only through the act of trading (which could also be called market-making) and reflect nothing other than this contingent event. Although Ayache does not himself say this, we may consider the price that any trade reveals for a traded derivative as a unique *name or designation* for that event, rather than as a number that belongs to any sort of series, however statistically chaotic, volatile, or complicated. In Ayache's own case, this leads him to a strong argument about trading as closely connected to writing, that is to the making of written agreements between traders who commit to an act of buying and selling.

Notice that, at one stroke, the severance of the price of the derivative from the universe of number, and thus of probability, renders the entire history of financial economics in its quantitative phase into the history of an error, even though it is a history with powerful effects (Barnesian counterperformative effects, as Donald MacKenzie would say) that have gradually come to dominate both theory and practice in the financial markets. In other words, most prior derivatives theorists and financial modelers (among them several Nobel Prize winners) and all their followers and internal debates become consigned to the domain of a massive mistake. It is hardly surprising that for the bulk of scholars in the study of finance, including those in the social studies of finance, Ayache is himself a Blank Swan, impossible to take seriously. A prominent exception is Nassim Taleb, who has endorsed Ayache's book, in spite of the fact that Ayache sees Taleb as having, in the end, failed to break out of the prison of probabilistic reasoning himself.

Let us consider, if nothing else for the purposes of our own speculative argument, where Ayache's effort to break out of the prison house of probability takes him. There are four interconnected directions in which Ayache wishes to take his reader, each of which has important implications for my own interest in bringing Weber and Durkheim back into the center of a new understanding of derivatives. The first involves market-making, the second involves writing, the third involves liquidity, and the fourth, and to my mind most important, involves the power of contingency over probability as a market creating force.

Ayache is at pains to argue that the market, so far as financial tools are concerned, is not a reflective or post hoc process for aggregating, mediating, or commensurating buyers and sellers (or demand and supply). Rather, it is a creative force, an ontological absolute that precedes and is the condition of all pricing. In this regard, Ayache does not refer to Durkheim, but his argument is a radical version of Durkheim's view on the prior ontological reality of society, in his famous argument in *The Elementary Forms of the Religious Life* (1995) about the social basis of the category of the sacred. In chapter 4, I have argued that the market today is remarkably similar to what society was for Durkheim, a reality that represented a moral force that could only be felt by humans as sacred, the force that made them comply with norms and experience their sociality as both larger and more abstract than their empirical, embodied selves. Ayache, in this sense, is a Durkheimian without being aware of this fact. The link between Ayache and Durkheim makes us aware that we need to look again at the logic of ritual action from a Durkheimian point of view, as proposed in previous chapters, in order to grasp the force of the derivative trade. In that chapter, I argued that the classical view of ritual logic saw it as a hedging logic that served the function of bringing routine and predictability to social life. After Austin's analysis of the "performative" as a speech act, anthropologists began to see that the force of ritual had to do with the way in which words were used in it to produce social effects. Subsequently, Judith Butler's work on performativity opened the door to the idea of retro-performativity. In turn, looking at ritual through the lens of retro-performativity makes it possible to see that ritual has the capacity to produce certainty in social life because it changes the terms in which uncertainty is understood.

So with this angle on ritual, as a co-staging of the relationship between uncertainty and certainty, with an underlying logic of retro-performativity, let us return to Ayache's view of the trading event as a critical moment in the making of markets through the contingent claim embodied by the agreed-upon price.

To better understand where Ayache's idea of the market and Durkheim's idea of society can come into fruitful juxtaposition, we need to look more closely at Ayache's view of the market (by which he means the financial market, and especially the market for derivatives, and not all markets). The key elements of Ayache's view of the market are inextricably tied up with his views of writing, contingent claims, the body of the trader, and the importance of price. Of these elements, the most important is his understanding of price, which he distinguishes radically from value. More precisely, he stresses that pricing, rather than valuation, is the key to the market in derivatives. This view of pricing leads him to a consistent and thorough critique of all stochastic models, methods, and accounts of the exchange of derivatives. In fact, exchange is the key market event for Ayache, in the sense that it is the event that cannot occur without the bodily actions of the trader, and in particular the ability of the trader to *negotiate a price in a written act of exchange.* This view of the priority of exchange over value (i.e., exchange creates value and not vice versa) is convergent with Simmel's view of exchange, which was also the framework for my own early argument (Appadurai 1986) about the tournament of value in the social life of things. Put another way, for Ayache the core of the value of the derivative is its *tradability*, reflected in its price, which has nothing to do with any specific quality or givenness about its underlying assets.

This emphasis on the retro-performativity of the trading event is what for Ayache characterizes the event. Ayache's view of the trading of the derivative—the quintessential market event, is best seen in section 7.1.2 (2010, 164–66) of his book of which a key section reads as follows:

> Therefore, to trade the derivative at variance with its value $V(S, t)$ is to enact the fact the probability distribution could have been different, which is to say that the probabilistic law of evolution of the underlying could have been different. This is not the same as the observation that the law *has* changed *from the start.* (From the start it was a contingent claim, not just a derivative.) It is from the start that the invention of the derivative and its trading fate and destination commit us to the thought that the probabilistic law could, and therefore should, be varied. The event of the trading of the derivative (when it is decided by the subject) retro-acts on the decision as to what the initial possibilities should have been in the first place. The trading event is a *grave* event, in the sense of *bringing about the possibilities that will have led to it.* Therefore the possibilities were not totalized after all. What should have been totalized are not only the different paths of the underlying but all the different possible probability weightings they can be assigned. We have to totalize all the different probabilistic laws, that is to say, all the alternative worlds in which the underlying evolves according to some fixed probabilistic laws.

This dense passage contains all the key elements of Ayache's ideas about contingency, price, value, trading, and the market, as well as his radical reasons for rejecting all stochastic, probabilistic, and even numerically driven accounts of the derivative. When we combine this view of the trading event with Ayache's account of the body of the trader and of the importance of writing as the key tool for the making of contingent claims, we can see the possibilities for a deep convergence between Durkheim's ideas about "collective effervescence" and Ayache's idea of the trading event as the real site of market-making through agreements about price. The deep link here is between the trading floor or space (even when it is virtual or machine-mediated) and those of the moment of collective effervescence in the ritual life of Australian aboriginal societies. The shared element is the electricity, the metasocial sensation of belonging, and the deep identifications (body-to-body) that attend the creation of society in ritual (for Durkheim) and the creation of the market through trading (for Ayache).

Durkheim's observations about collective effervescence, based largely on the work of earlier observers of the corroboree ceremony among certain aboriginal populations of Northern Australia, is an important part of his effort to understand the force and significance of totemic emblems (largely of plants and animals) in the social life of these Australian societies. It is well known that this analysis of totemic names, emblems, and ritual processes is a central part of Durkheim's argument about the ways in which the abstraction that is in fact society is concretized as the sacred, and how this logic of giving sacred status to specific names, things, and categories is in fact a more general way in which the social is displaced and misrecognized, in all human societies, as the sacred or as God. Durkheim realized that a strictly semiotic analysis of the correspondences between totemic emblems and social categories (such as clans, phratries) would fail to analyze the force, the conviction, the awe, and the attachment that these emblems provoke and promote in these societies.

For this, he needed to rework earlier descriptions of certain key collective ritual elements of aboriginal societies, which occurred when these typically small, scattered groups, preoccupied with the humdrum tasks of hunting and gathering, came into larger collectivities and encountered the force of their social connectivity in bigger scales and in unusual, intensified circumstances. These special moments, spaces, and contexts were, for Durkheim, the moments in which the awesome force of the social, as something that lies both inside and outside the individuals who compose it, is nurtured, materialized and energized. It is a well-known fact that this part of Durkheim's analysis is the inspiration of most serious analysis of ritual processes ever since (starting with Mauss and others who worked with Durkheim, up to and including Geertz, Turner, and other major recent analysts of ritual processes). Lévi-Strauss, famously, took up a more cerebral and cognitivist strand in Durkheim's thought and ended up making the Durkheimian "savage" more cerebral than Durkheim may have wished.

The following passage from *The Elementary Forms of Religious Life* (1995) captures how Durkheim saw the role of collective effervescence in major ritual events as key to the making of aboriginal society:

> It is in these effervescent social milieus, and indeed from that very effervescence, that the religious idea seems to have been born. That such is indeed the origin tends to be confirmed by the fact that what is properly called religious activity in Australia is almost entirely contained within the periods when these gatherings are held. To be sure, there is no society among whom the great cult ceremonies are not more or less periodic, but in the more advanced societies, there is virtually no day on which some prayer or offering is not offered to the Gods or on which some ritual obligation is not fulfilled. (220)

The brief section of Durkheim's most important work on the social basis of religiosity is disproportionately important to his understanding of the dynamics of the social in ritual life and of the capacity of collective effervescence to produce that sort of conviction, force, and electricity (the latter two terms coming from Durkheim's own usage), which does not only symbolize or represent the presence of society as the ruling force that links and regulates the bodies of its members. It also generates that sense of belonging to a powerful and abstract force, simultaneously ecstatic and regulated, which lends its authority to the profane moments, spaces, and contexts of quotidian social life outside the ritual sphere. In this sense, rituals are not simply performative (in the sense of Austin and many later anthropological followers of Austin) but are in fact constitutive or, better still, generative of the force of all social conventions in ordinary social life. In fact, it would not be exaggeration to suggest that a close reading of the section on collective effervescence as part of the larger argument of *The Elementary Forms of Religious Life* (1995) as being a strong argument for what we might regard today as a kind of retroperformativity, a speech act, ritual act, or formalized sequence of action that takes effect not just by meeting the conditions of felicity but in fact by creating and recreating these very conditions through the ritual act itself. This is the only way in which Durkheim could explain the excess of force, conviction, and authority that rituals of this type produce, beyond what could be produced by any sort of logic of representation, equivalence, or legitimation that religious symbols might otherwise have for the social categories which they instantiate and motivate.

This view of Durkheim's analysis of collective effervescence allows us to return to my earlier argument about the replacement of society by market in the contemporary world, nowhere clearer than in the world of derivatives. Here we need to recall Ayache's view of the market as constituted by the immanent reality of contingent claims through which interacting trading bodies create prices and thus create a market that always exceeds the predictions or projections of any stochastic or probabilistic model of prior events.

At this stage it is important to recognize that contemporary trading floors and markets for derivatives are not simple corroborees, that traders are not our version of effervescent aboriginals, and that the processes of abstraction involved in society and market are nowhere perfectly congruent, even in our contemporary financialized world. Nor am I proposing that the Durkheimian view of collective effervescence is a warrant for the numerous invocations of "irrational exuberance" and other tropes of emotional excess that have dogged recent narratives about the financial markets and their chief actors.

What is true is that the derivatives market retro-engineers its own conditions of possibility by bringing together the contingent claims of traders whose agreements are solely expressed in prices, and in prices whose logic is precisely to create a variance between price and value (as described by any and all stochastic models). In this, Ayache's market and Durkheim's corroboree have an important point of convergence, in that they add something *rule-governed and simultaneously unpredictable* to the governing model of their respective environments, society, and the market respectively. In both cases, the ritualized encounter produces its own conditions of possibility. The quotidian sense that society, or the market, operates according to legitimate, predictable, and shared laws is only produced in those ecstatic moments in which actions are taken that expand the boundaries of propriety in a manner that can be safe if and only if the prior, quotidian workings of society (or market) were in fact saturated with that sense of conviction, force, and energy that their ritual production actually creates!

This equation throws a new light on some fundamental issues that interest all analysts of financial markets, the most relevant being those coming out of the early work of Frank Knight on risk and uncertainty. The reading I have offered of Ayache's recent book places it in a line of descent from Durkheim's 1912 observations about collective effervescence in the ritual life of Australian aboriginal societies in the late nineteenth century. The major interpretive claim I take from Ayache is that the complete domination of financial economics since 1973 (when the Black-Scholes model of options pricing effected a permanent quantitative revolution in this field), by probabilistic and stochastic models for analyzing and predicting action in financial markets, was a huge step in the wrong direction. Among the many implications of Ayache's argument, a major one involves risk and uncertainty, which in Ayache's view does not flow from any discernible study of trends, patterns, or outcomes in these markets, in spite of the Barnesian performativity arguments of MacKenzie and others.

While Ayache's work may be questioned, debated, or even dismissed on technical or stylistic grounds in present or future debates, a critical part of his descriptive argument is about the role of what he calls contingent claims in the constitution of prices through trading events in the market, which Ayache sees as acquiring their status only because they deviate in unpredictable ways from any and all predictions of the future based on stochastic models of past events. All that we have are a succession of *prices*, which are in fact unique outcomes of contingent claims between traders, and whose quantitative form does not imply that they are parts of any coherent numerical series.

If Ayache is right that prices are only accidentally expressed numerically but do not belong to any quantitatively readable series at all, then the actions of traders are in fact creative efforts, in written agreements, to create prices for derivatives, and such prices are *the sole instantiation* of the market. Further, in their continuous becoming, they also create, retrospectively, the entire set of the conditions, which allows them to come into being without being in any reliable way derivable from them. Price does not rest on any discernible metric of prior value, but is the mechanism through which the market continuously rewrites the past in a manner that allows for new prices to be set and thus for the market in derivatives to move forward.

If the essence of what Ayache's traders do is make agreements and name prices (give names to derivatives in the form of quantities), what they are doing can also be described in terms of the corroboree model used by Durkheim to describe the peculiar relationship of the rituals of Australian Aboriginals to the conditions of quotidian social life, which are continuously re-energized and reauthorized by these events of collective effervescence, and are in not in any sense (stochastic or historical) outcomes of prior quotidian events.

Here Ayache's reading of the role of the trading event as producing each price as a unique product, and not as a member of a series, offers up a new way to read Durkheim's path-breaking observation about the significance of totemic names and objects in Australian aboriginal religion. Durkheim's breakthrough was to see that totemic groupings used the names of specific animal and plant species to represent the identity of human social groups (such as the clan) in a manner that simultaneously externalized and cosmologized the power of clan identity, apart from and in spite of the transient, fluctuating, and small number of actual groups that wandered in the Australian desert in the quotidian work of hunting and reproduction. As we have seen, Durkheim also recognized the role of collective effervescence—the embodied social electricity—produced in the periodic ritual gatherings such as corroborees, in which the truth of society was felt, embodied, and collectively produced. We might say, following Ayache, and recognizing what Durkheim himself did not see, that the collective effervescence of these collective ritual occasions was precisely a product of the co-staging of uncertainty and certainty, in a ritual process that literally produced the totemic identities of social groups and reproduced the idea of social collectivity that transcended all quotidian social groupings.

The collective effervescence of the trading floor or—in electronically mediated environments—of the trading network is, just as the corroboree is for the Durkheimian analysis of aboriginal religion, the moment when certainty is produced out of uncertainty, but in both cases it is *not because the ritual event produces ritual certainty out of raw social uncertainty* but because social uncertainty is already recast in the ritual process by the very agreement of all actors to participate and collaborate in the ritual process. Thus the power of a successful ritual, which works when its presupposition that all the collaborating actors are indeed appropriate participants in the ritual that was successfully enacted, is to confirm that society (in the case of the Aboriginals) and the market (in the case of traders) can indeed be made to appear in and through the ritual process and through its transformation of uncertainty to certainty *within the ritual (or trading) frame itself.*

In other words, what Ayache allows us to bring to Durkheim is a nonfunctionalist view of the relationship of collective effervescence in the ritual process to the experience of totemic groupings as the abstract elements of a coherent social totality. Just as the traders produce, one pricing agreement at a time, a repeated certainty that there is a market as opposed to no market at all, so the large-scale ritual events in aboriginal society regularly produce the certainty that there is society as a large impersonal and ethical force in aboriginal life and not just a scattered encounter of small, quotidian social groupings. In this regard, the totemic emblems serve exactly like Ayache's prices that appear in one form (a numerical or natural series) but actually embody the force of the very totality (society or market) that they presuppose for their actions to succeed.

Put even more generally, if derivatives, as written agreements about contingent claims, do not emerge from any prior distribution or trend of pricing events, it is the trade that creates the price rather than vice versa. This reversal makes the embodied action of traders who agree to any trade the source of the ever-emerging market, and it makes no sense to attempt to read the market in terms of stochastic trends of any sort. This point of view has two important implications. The first is that the relationship between risk and uncertainty (whatever the model, Knightian, Brownian, or other) could play out in a very different space than the one we had previously imagined. The second implication is that trading events take their force not from any sort of quantitative feature of the price but of its written force, the force of a contingent agreement. I consider these two implications below, and do so by rereading of Weber's views on charisma and bureaucracy.

On the first implication: if Ayache is right about the trading event as price-generating, about price as the only material fact of consequence in the derivatives market, and about the irrelevance of stochastic models to market processes, *the very locus of risk shifts.* The true risk of each and every derivative trade would lie not in the space of the stochastic patterns, which we can read into the past, but in the willingness of traders to come to agreements on the pricing of derivatives on the floor, in the living environment of the emerging market. The true risk is the risk of arriving at an agreement on any sort of contingent claim (from traders on either side of a transaction) expressed as a price, in the absence of any reliable stochastic or probabilistic model of prior prices. The true ritual risk is the risk that those preconditions that the exchanges that the ritual context aim to produce fail to do so. In the environment of ritual performances, this means that allies who were expected to behave in a certain manner during the uncertain real-time unfolding of the ritual process do not do so (for any number of reasons, which may be social, political, personal, or accidental). In the trading environment, if an agreement is not achieved, its market-making potential is transactionally squandered.

Risk in this perspective is certainly not anything measurable, predictable, or quantifiable from prior data about underlying assets or any other historical indicator. Risk is about whether or not an agreement about a certain price will emerge *at all*. In other words, the real risk of trading in derivatives is the risk that any specific effort to make a market for a derivative, or to find someone who agrees to negotiate on a price, will have no result at all. In this instance risk is exactly the same as uncertainty, both being ways to talk about the nonquantifiable unknown about whether any counterparty at all to a potential agreement could be found. The risk is not about the end of the day, when traders, their managers, and their firms total up the bottom line of actual trades. Rather, the risk is contained *in every effort* by any trader to make a written agreement, in Ayache's sense of the term. It is simply immeasurable by any quantitative means. This amounts to saying that in regard to such trades, risk and uncertainty have no practical difference. This is one real implication of Ayache's bold effort to say that we misunderstand prices when we regard them as numbers, which behave as members of any temporal set.

This takes us into the second implication of Ayache's insight, which concerns writing and agreements. The fact that this risk is about whether or not a trader can produce a pricing agreement with another trader to create a derivative event takes its force from the domain of writing, as Ayache would put it. In my opinion, the emphasis on writing in Ayache takes him in a misleading direction, which stresses surfaces (rather than stochastic depths), and produces the most tenuous strand of his argument, which is the analogy between originality in the realm of writing and in the realm of trading, with complex readings of Badiou, Meillasoux, Baudrillard, and others to sustain his extended allegorical claim. What Ayache is right about is the importance of the written agreement to all exchange in the historical period of the emergence of the contract, which as a social form relies not only on writing, but also on the law and in particular on the enforceability of all contracts, including commercial contacts through a combination of legal and bureaucratic institutions that allow contingent claims to achieve the historical status of market transactions about actual commodities or assets (prior to their rendition into derivatives). This brings us, once again, to Max Weber.

Let us recall that Max Weber was throughout his working life tormented by the tension between the charismatic and the routinized dimensions of modern social life. This tension was a critical element of his writings about leadership, status, and power, but it was also a central element of his arguments about salvation, election, magic, and other features of many religions, and was also a noteworthy feature of his understanding of economic action in the realm of accumulation, warfare, and entrepreneurship. We can summarize Weber's preoccupation between the domain of charisma and routinization as lying in the fact that he understood that a world entirely devoid of one of these elements would be unthinkable. Without charisma there would be no new movements, enterprises, or alterations of existing societies. Without routinization there would be no secure mechanisms for reproducing hard-won new ideas for the organization of economy, polity, or society. The tension between charisma and routine—in politics, economy, religion, and law—could be said to be the primary tension in all of Weber's work.

The problem of how charisma in fact enters human affairs, and the ways in which its role has changed through human history, led Weber, certainly in his pessimistic later years, to believe that routinization, in the form of rationalization through law, bureaucracy, and economy, had perhaps gone too far, and this is what led him to his famous "iron cage" reference. For this, Weber and many of his later followers laid much of the blame on money, on the market, and on economic rationalization in general.

Yet, it is possible to reconsider the problem of charisma in social life, if we take the point of view, following Ayache, that sees the trading event as quintessentially outside the realm of stochastic processes, and sees traders as market-makers who rely on the power of the contingent, written claim on tradable derivatives through the eternal unpredictability of price. This view of the trading event, as one that retrospectively and continuously creates its own conditions of possibility, also resonates, as I have argued, with Durkheim's insight about the centrality of collective effervescence at the heart of major ritual processes in which societies perform their own sociality and experience its electricity, its force, and its apparently transcendental authority. If we are right to make this link between Durkheim and Ayache, and right also that the greatest risk taken by all traders exchanging derivatives in the unfolding market is *the risk that they will ever find a counterparty*, and only secondarily about the profit or loss involved in any given trade, we have a new way to connect Durkheim's idea of collective effervescence and Weber's view of charisma.

In this revisionist view, inspired by Ayache's argument that financial derivatives achieve their greatest force by escaping the logic of all numerically patterned stochastic processes, by capturing radical contingency in every act of contingent claim-making reflected in a price-based derivative trade, the temporal and logical relationship between the moments of charisma and the moment of routine is completely transformed. Seen this way, the charismatic trade neither emerges from the predictable, chartable, or quantifiable nature of prior trends, nor does it settle back into routine economic activity, through the work of investors, shareholders, or regulators. Rather, the charismatic nature of the trading event continuously lends its collective effervescence, *retrospectively*, to the entire structure of rules, valuations, agreements, and institutions that surround it, in the remainder of the market, outside the space of the traded derivative. In other words, the realm of derivatives trading is a continuous source of collective effervescence, which energizes the underlying instruments from which its own value is allegedly derived. Thus, derivative trading is the source of charismatic energy in the contemporary market, with the added new feature that it energizes the more quotidian activities of the market in a retrospective manner, just as collective effervescence in aboriginal ritual lends its electricity to the profane social formations that are its own conditions of possibility.

Thus, just as the true risk in the ritual process is that the conditions of felicity that are presupposed in it will somehow fail or be violated, so the true risk of any derivative trading event is that the contingent claim reflected in any price proposal will find no counterparty and thus no trade will actually occur. Risk, in this sense, suffuses the entire trading process and is not truly to be found in the statistical profile of any particular trade. Just as the collective effervescence of the ritual cannot be understood outside of the risk of ritual failure, so the charismatic potential of any trading event cannot be found outside of the risk that a counterparty may not be found at all and thus the contingent claim will come to naught. The risk is of absolute failure rather than of a statistically measurable likelihood of failure. This is the potential power of Ayache's claim that we should shift our understanding of derivative trading entirely outside the realm of probability.

Behind many of the debates about the financial debacle of 2008 and the approximately three decades of legal and technical innovation in the financial markets that led to it (Black-Scholes to today) is a debate about the derivative form itself. On the one side stand the vast majority of financial actors, policymakers, and apologists, who see derivatives as remarkable instruments for the creation of real wealth, primarily because they serve to guarantee and increase liquidity for the financial markets and thus assure the rapid and efficient flow of finance to those sectors of industry, technology, and production that most need this wealth. In this argument, every effort to restrict or regulate the derivatives market is a brake on liquidity and the disproportionate profits of the major banks and funds and the huge salaries and bonuses of finance professionals are their just reward for taking those risks that promote such liquidity. On the other side stand a heterogeneous group of critics, ranging from those who wish to bring more transparency and more responsible thresholds of leverage for traders to those, such as critics in the Occupy movement, who wish to shrink or abolish the financial markets altogether. Between these two sides stand a vast range of opinions about how and to what extent the financial markets should be regulated, so as to optimize the relationship between liquidity and social equity.

If the analysis proposed in this chapter has any validity, and if it can be worked out more fully, we stand to gain a new understanding of the nature of real risk in financial markets and in particular of risk in derivatives trading. If the real source of risk in these instruments lies not in the stochastics of risk and return in the trading of these instruments but, in fact, in the likelihood that any radically contingent claim may or may not be honored, then we could begin to develop an analysis in which liquidity is not generated by derivatives because they allow new wealth to be generated that did not exist before. Rather, every trade in derivatives is a charismatic event that retrospectively increases the deeper legitimacy of the market as a whole by a continuous chain of retrospective validations outside the realm of stochastic processes and more squarely within the realm of the written agreement, the contract, and the contingent claim. If the true value of the derivative form is to provide a continuous and reliable source of collective effervescence through which the valuation of underlying assets can be enhanced and leveraged, we may have here a different engine of wealth creation than we had previously imagined. If we are able to analyze the dynamics of this engine more creatively, it might lead us to recognize that derivatives can indeed be socially accessible forms of vast new wealth, but only if their charismatic properties are more carefully recognized, socialized, and governed.

CHAPTER SEVEN

THE WEALTH OF DIVIDUALS

Finance and Dividualization

One of the pernicious effects of the era of financialization has been the erosion of the status of the individual.[1] By this I do not mean simply that the individual has been alienated, dispossessed, exploited, mystified, or marginalized, though there is some truth to each of these claims. But there is nothing new about this order of social cost paid for the benefits of industrial capitalism.

I am referring to a more radical and less visible process whereby the broad social canvas in which the Western individual (both as category and as social fact) dominated society has been eroded and thinned out in favor of a more elementary level of social agency, which some have called the "dividual." The dividual is not an elementary particle (or homunculus) of the individual but something more like the material substrate from which the individual emerges, the precursor and precondition of the individual, more protean and less easy to discern and to name than the individual, which is one of its structural products.

I hope to show that the erosion of the individual and the rise of the dividual is largely an effect of the workings of financial capitalism since the early 1970s and in particular a collateral effect of the spread of the derivative form as the quintessential tool of making money out of uncertainty in this era of financialization. The form of dividualism produced by financial capital is ideal for the masking of inequality, for the multiplication of opaque quantitative forms that are illegible to the average citizen, and for the multiplication of profit-making tools and techniques, which can escape audit, regulation, and social control. In short, the dividualism that financialization both presumes and enhances is counter to the interests of the large majority of society. But it is also irreversible. Thus, rather than argue for a return to the era of the composite (or canonic, or classical) individual, I propose a new form of politics, which can create radically new forms of collective agency and connectivity that can replace the current predatory forms of dividualism with truly socialized dividualism. To make this journey, one needs a fuller understanding of the idea of the dividual.

To think the dividual, we must unthink the individual. This is no easy task, but one way to understand the post-Enlightenment conception of the individual, on which much ink has been spilled, is to see it as the crystallized product of many centuries of gradual convergence in the West between the idea of the actor, the agent, the person, the self, the human soul, and the human being. Each of these categories can be provided with a distinct Western genealogy, composed of elements that can be traced back variously to the Greeks, the Romans, the Christians, the Jews, and a multitude of subtraditions, countertraditions, and hybrid traditions that have grown up around these major traditions. With Descartes and his idea of the *cogito* and its resident "I," the basis was laid for these ideas to be amalgamated to the point of mutual fungibility. Starting in the eighteenth century, it became hard to set apart ideas of humanity, agency, personality, and selfhood, which only recently have begun to reveal their contingent and composite architecture. This was all the more forcefully naturalized as the dominant Western ideas of property, political voice, wealth, and market interests all began to reinforce the idea that some sort of individual was the isomorphic site of agency, natural rights, biological coherence, and moral value. The individual become the invisible condition of possibility for all Western political, economic, and moral thought.

Anthropology as a discipline was well situated to unravel this composite idea of the individual at the beginning of the twentieth century, as its practitioners encountered ideas of soul, technique, religion, and politics that appeared not to revolve around the idea of the individual that Western ethnographers and scholars had come to view as natural and universal. Still, it was fairly late in the twentieth century when two very different anthropological giants, Marcel Mauss (1985) and Meyer Fortes (1973), dealt separate blows to the common sense about the universality of the individual. Mauss was the most important pupil (and nephew) of Durkheim and is arguably the single most important thinker of the founding period of anthropology for all anthropologists today. Fortes was a giant in the mid-century context of British social anthropology, whose primary concern was with the ways in which individuals and collectivities were formed through other entities which he, for the first time in the history of anthropology, used the term "dividual," in 1973. Mauss deserves the credit for distinguishing the category of the person from that of the self, the latter in his view being not a social artifact but a moral one. But Fortes identified the "dividual" as a more elementary and foundational element of agency (both human and animal) than the individual. For this he deserves credit.

But the most important figure, and the least remembered, at least in this regard, is McKim Marriott, who in the early 1970s at the University of Chicago formulated a theory of the "dividual" that was the most explicit, radical, and generative statement of the relativity and parochialism of our own naturalized idea of the individual in the West. Marriott, in collaboration with a younger historian at Chicago, Ronald Inden, wrote an important essay (1974) that built upon the earlier work of David Schneider on "code" and "substance" in American kinship, to offer a radical new theory of South Asian caste systems, which had hitherto been seen as extreme versions of Western social forms such as class and race. Synthesizing a vast array of empirical ethnographic studies of rural South Asia, as well as a variety of historical, philosophical, and religio-legal sources from the archive of Indic civilization, Marriott and Inden argued that South Asian social systems were built on a wholly different architecture from those of the West, whose foundation was the "dividual," an agent of action and transaction that was continually transferred by contact with other dividuals to create new arrays of rank, purity, and potential liberation from the material world. This idea emerged as part of a debate between Marriott and Louis Dumont, whose path-breaking study of caste, *Homo Hierarchicus* (1970), had made the case for a radical contrast between Western individualism and Indic holism, without any reference to the idea of the "dividual." Much later, Marilyn Strathern (1988) made an ostensibly independent discovery of the idea of the "dividual" and generated a substantial Melanesian dialogue about this category, which was oddly indifferent to its earlier anthropological lineages.

Entirely outside of the anthropological tradition, we have another emergent line of thought, best articulated by Gilles Deleuze, who developed a radical cosmology of rhizomic networks, man-machine assemblages, and nomadic social forms with its roots in Bergson and Spinoza (Deleuze and Guattari 1987). Deleuze's thought, partly developed in collaboration with the psychoanalyst Felix Guattari, ranged from studies of ecology and biopolitics to studies of cinema and the unconscious, which were regarded with the greatest of respect by his major contemporaries, such as Foucault and Derrida. The implications of Deleuze's ideas about energy, machinic forms, and human agency are only now beginning to be fully explored, notably in what are now referred to as the "new materialisms."[2] Deleuze's ontology may be described as dynamic, vitalist, and processual, and constitutes a radical metaphysical critique of the Cartesian world-picture. Especially in its linkage of the vitalist tradition of Spinoza and Bergson to current interests in machinic agency and ecopolitics, Deleuze is the crucial link. It is noteworthy that the only explicit reference to the "dividual" in Deleuze's oeuvre occurs in a short and prescient article published in English in 1992, where Deleuze distinguished what he calls the emerging societies of control from what were earlier disciplinary societies (with explicit reference to Foucault). Deleuze draws the distinction in many dimensions but especially when he says:

We no longer find ourselves dealing with the mass/individual pair. Individuals have become "*dividuals*," and masses, samples, data, markets, or "banks." Perhaps it is money that expresses the distinction between the two societies best, since discipline always referred back to minted money that locks gold as numerical standard, while control relates to floating rates of exchange, modulated according to a rate established by a set of standard currencies. The old monetary mole is the animal of the space of enclosure, but the serpent is that of the societies of control. We have passed from one animal to the other, from the mole to the serpent, in the system under which we live, but also in our manner of living and in our relations with others. The disciplinary man was a discontinuous producer of energy, but the man of control is undulatory, in orbit, in a continuous network. Everywhere surfing has already replaced the older sports. (1992)

Though this statement by Deleuze is even more compressed and aphoristic than is usual for him, it allows us to recognize the momentous way in which contemporary finance has produced (or at least catalyzed) a dramatically contemporary form of the dividual, which is directly linked to quantification in all its pervasive forms, one of which is monetization. *What contemporary finance does is to monetize all the other forms of quantification that surround us today, by taking advantage of the dividual forms that such quantification continuously produces.* To move from the idea of the dividual to an argument about contemporary finance, requires three steps: (a) examining the way in which finance has created a predatory mode of dividuation; (b) showing how the idea of the dividual illuminates the workings of ritual in precapitalist societies and (c) demonstrating that this dividualized ritual logic underpins the social form of the derivative and can be used to move from predatory dividuation to progressive dividuation. These steps are the subjects of the next three sections.

The Subprime Mortgage and Predatory Dividuation

We have already looked briefly at the nature of the mortgage form and its role in the crisis of 2007–8 in previous chapters. The bizarreness of this form of mediated financial materiality has only risen to public attention because of the meltdown of 2008, in which new forms of bundled mortgage derivatives played a massive role in the market collapse, the effects of which are still very much with us.[3]

Housing loans (mortgages) are an essential part of the material life of financial objects in the United States because they take a mythic element of the contemporary cosmology of capitalism, in which your "own" house is treated as the mark of financial adulthood and security, all housing values are always supposed to rise, and though what you own is a piece of paper, you are led to believe that you actually own a house. The bizarre materiality of the mortgage-backed American house is that while its visible material form is relatively fixed, bounded, and indivisible, its financial form, the mortgage, has now been structured to be endlessly divisible, recombinable, saleable, and leverage-able for financial speculators, in a manner that is both mysterious and toxic.

The fact is that this financial rematerialization of the American home is made possible not merely through the mechanism of the mortgage (which is, after all, simply a particularly complex long-term loan) but through the most complex form of financial mediation the world has known, the derivative. The global financial crisis of 2008 was in no small part created by the crash of housing prices (of the underlying commodity, in other words), which had been leveraged into a complex and massive set of traded derivatives whose values were out of all proportion to the actual value of homes. This yawning gap between home values and derivative prices was in large part due to the creation of certain derivatives, which allowed a large number of subprime mortgages to be made to first-time home-owners. The big question about the mortgage crisis of 2007–8, which was a primary driver of the financial meltdown of that year in the United States, is: why did so many banks make so many weak or risky loans?

The answer is that in the decades that preceded the global financial crisis, and especially after 1990, the housing market was identified by the financial industries as being capable of yielding far more potential wealth than it had historically done through the mediation of new derivative instruments. The principal two new instruments that allowed banks to do this were mortgage-backed securities (MBS), which are a specific form of something called asset-backed securities (ABS). These securities allowed "bundling" of large numbers of mortgages into a single tradable instrument whose value depended on different ideas about the future value of such bundles between buyers and sellers. This bundling also had another feature: subprime mortgages could be bundled together with mortgages with superior credit ratings and, with the connivance of the credit rating agencies, toxic loans were in effect laundered by bundling them together with better loans, disguising them under an overall superior rating. This meant that many lenders could make money by originating subprime loans so that they could be bundled and resold by being mixed in with higher quality loans. A second derivative instrument that enabled this dangerous alchemy was called a collateralized default obligation (CDO), which allowed these bundles of mortgages to be divided into tranches or levels that had different credit ratings. What is important, though technically a shade more obscure, is how the higher value tranches were used to bury, obscure, or disguise the more toxic tranches.

Imagine selling a house with a beautiful view from the upper floor and a leaky basement, which is hidden from view by some mysterious financial instrument that groups all the houses and uses the grading of the top stories to disguise all the leaky basements. This is what allowed the trading of mortgage-based securities and collateralized debt obligations to be a roaring business through the first few years of this millennium, riding the wave that the rising value of all housing would indefinitely postpone the flooding of many millions of basements. Well, housing prices did eventually fall precipitously and the metaphorical basements did flood, leaving hundreds of lenders holding toxic assets and hundreds of homeowners holding mortgages (rightly called underwater mortgages) on which they owed more to the bank than the house was currently worth. And because these and other derivative instruments connected the massive collapse of the mortgage market to all other credit markets, the entire financial system of the United States was on the brink of disaster until the government pumped in a vast amount of public funds to secure this avalanche of bad loans and debts, in the first weeks of the new Obama administration.

So what is the moral of this story for our purposes today? The moral is that the derivative is above all a new form of mediation. What it mediates by the endless exploitation of the spreads between emergent prices and the unknown future values of commodities is the always-evolving distance between the commodity and the asset, the latter being the commodity as its unrealized potential for future profit. In this process, derivatives are not mere financial instruments (however exotic). They are practices of mediation, which yield new materialities, in this case the materialities of the asset, which are potentially available in all commodities. Notice how far this chain of mediations has brought us from the house as a simple materiality. Mediated in the capitalist market, the house becomes the mortgage; further mediated, the mortgage becomes an asset, itself subject to trading as an uncertainly priced future commodity. Mediated yet again, this asset becomes part of an asset-backed security, a new derivative form, which can be further exchanged in its incarnation as a debt-obligation. At every step, the financial form serves as mediating practice, which produces a new order of materiality. Notice that in our current financial world this iterative chain of financial derivations also affects other materialities, apart from housing, such as food, health, education, energy, the environment, and virtually everything else that can be mediated into new forms of materiality. So the home—as a material fact—does not exist in our highly financialized world apart from its availability to the mediation of the derivative form. Conversely, it is only by materializing new wealth out of assets such as housing, food, health, and education, among many other assets, that the mediating powers of the derivative become realized, and real.

The relationship between the mortgage crisis and the derivative form cannot fully be understood without understanding the much more radical and widespread way in which financialization relies on a variety of forms of quantification of the person that correspond precisely to Deleuze's (1992) idea of the dividual in societies of control.

There are, of course, other scoring tools in wide use in American society for a variety of purposes, ranging from security alerts to SAT examinations to various insurance protocols for defining risk properties to pools of customers. This issue was discussed in the argument of chapter 4 about personhood, quantification, and predatory dividualization. This feature of contemporary finance would be unviable except in the context of a sweeping process through which contemporary Western individuals have been rendered subjects of a vast array of data search, collation, pattern-seeking, and exploitation, some of which has been captured in the recent category of "Big Data."[4] Big data pervades the activities of the state, private corporate enterprises, and many varieties of security apparatus. Point-of-sale information has been mined for several decades to refine consumer demographics; point-of-use data is critical for the NSA's telephonic surveillance activities both within and outside the United States; social media companies generate troves of interactional information of value to both the state and to the corporate world.

It has been widely observed that these multiple and massive inventories of data are the object of complex new forms of pattern-seeking, mining, and strategic application. What has been less noticed is the tectonic shift that these data industries imply in the conception of the individual as the foundation of modern Western ethics, ontology, and epistemology. The most critical implication of these new forms of data gathering and analysis, for the present argument, is the ways in which they atomize, partition, qualify, and quantify the individual so as to make highly particular features of the individual subject or actor more important than the person as a whole. Numbers are attached to consumer purchases, discrete interactions, credit, life-chances, health profiles, educational test results, and a whole battery of related life events, so as to make these parts of the individual combinable and customizable in such ways as to render moot or irrelevant the idea of the "whole," the classical individual. This logic of dividuation has natural and historical roots in the machineries of insurance, risk management, and behavioral analysis that pool these quantified parts into larger quantified categories, which can then be further searched, combined, and reaggregated so as to maximize knowledge, profits, and risk minimization for various large-scale institutional actors who have no interest in the idiosyncrasies of the classical individual. I call this logic predatory because its interests are narrow and control-oriented, with no regard for individuals except as holding addresses for a large variety of dividual features and possibilities. Contemporary finance lies at the heart of these dividualizing techniques, because it relies on the management and exploitation of risks that are not the primary risks of ordinary individuals in an uncertain world, but the derivative or secondary risks that can be designed in the aggregation and recombination of large masses of dividualized behaviors and attributes from credit scores to SAT results.

The multiple derivative instruments that were developed by slicing and dicing individual mortgages so as to generate profit for financial institutions exemplify this predatory logic and have the effect of making dividualized actors incapable of any concerted critique, resistance, or reform with regard to these predatory logics. Thus the many varieties of antidebt movement (exemplified by the Occupy movement) are doomed to fail because they seek to oppose dividualizing logics with strategies of mobilization, persuasion, and critique, which rely on the politics of the individual. To create a strong politics to oppose the predatory dividualism that drives the current logic of the derivative requires an alternative approach to politics, a topic addressed in the concluding section of this chapter. But now we must consider the dividual logic that underpins classic precapitalist societies, largely unmonetized worlds whose approach to risk and uncertainty can be seen in their ritual machineries.

The Dividual in Ritual Societies

I have already shown that Durkheim's ideas about religion were radically secularizing and allow us to see the market as a sacralizing force in contemporary society. To link this argument to the idea of the dividual, we need to briefly recall the argument in chapter 5 about the history of anthropological work on the logic of ritual. I referred there to the well-established "hedging" view of ritual, which lives on today in the most colloquial uses of the word. I further proposed that the Austinian view of performatives was the most important innovation on this hedging view. Subsequently, Judith Butler's work introduced the idea of what I now refer to as retro-performativity, which allows us to see that ritual can be regarded as a framework for the co-staging of uncertainty and certainty in social life. I concluded that argument by referring to the classic work of Arnold van Gennep on *The Rites of Passage* (1960) and some of his modern followers about rituals with a sacrificial element, in which a person, or a part of the person, is sacrificed in the interest of reproducing a social and cosmological whole.

The logic of sacrifice can, in one important respect, illuminate all rituals, and that is in the way sacrifice relies on the critical role of dividuals in order to accomplish its goals. *Sacrifice can only work when what is offered, or given up, usually to a God or ancestor, is a dynamic part of some apparent whole.* In other words, the parts that are given up by one actor to another, in the world of precapitalist sacrifice, are dynamic parts, which also carry their own energies, vitalities, and strivings (in the sense that Spinoza used the term *conatus*). They are not inert shreds or samples of a prior whole. Consider the logic of sorcery, which frequently relies on human bodily leavings (such as nails, hair, skin, or other elements of an actor), to be operated on at a distance by the sorcerer, so as to provide malign or deadly effects on the original source of these leavings. Or consider offerings of human hair to enshrined deities in many parts of India, as gifts that are part of vows to these deities, ventured in the hope of receiving boons, such as a child for a barren woman. Many distinguished anthropologists, such as Lévi-Strauss (1976), Tambiah (1968), and Leach (1976), have pointed out that the efficacy of rituals relies on a special combination of the logics of metaphor (the partial likeness of unlike things) and the logic of metonym (contiguity, connectivity, participation) that connects parts to wholes: head to body, hair to head, organs to other organs, bodies to their effluvia. Metonym is no simple logic of part and whole. It is a logic of dividuation, in which personhood rests not in the stable crystallization of body, soul, intention, and affect in a single bodily envelope, but in the highly volatile relationship between those substances (flesh, blood, vitality, energy, essence, and effluvia) that are always in the process of interacting and recombining to produce temporary assemblages of sociality, identity, and affect. This is the dividual logic of noncapitalist societies described by McKim Marriott (1976), Marilyn Strathern (1988), and others who have followed them in the ethnography of South Asia, Melanesia, and other places outside the capitalist orbit. This is dividuation without exploitation because it lacks the monetized and predatory logic by which the derivative form exploits the *dividuation of the many for the individuation (by profit-making) of the few.*

Indeed, if we look more closely at retro-performativity, now widely regarded as the underlying logic of many ritual worlds, it can be shown that dividuation is the underlying condition of possibility of retro-performativity in ritual. Because this argument is not a familiar or generally accepted view among anthropologists, it requires an explicit argument. Let us look at the classic instance of the gift (*le don*), first made a canonic concern of anthropology by Marcel Mauss, and then elaborated and debated by a distinguished sequence of French thinkers, including Claude Lévi-Strauss, Emile Benveniste, Pierre Bourdieu, Helene Cixous, Luce Irigiray, and Jacques Derrida, as well as a host of ethnographers and ethnologists working in other academic traditions on a large range of noncapitalist societies.[5]

The idea of retro-performativity, which has recurred throughout this book, amounts in its essence to the following: ritual has its most powerful effect by bringing into effect a change of state in its prime actors as well as in the cosmology that is its frame by realizing (making real) a world presumed as its precondition through a sequence of actions in which effects create causes or conditions of possibility that take shape only in retrospect. This retro-creativity (or -performativity) has hitherto been seen primarily as a linguistic effect, which is a temporal reversal of the logic of the performative first identified by Austin with regard to utterances, which change the world by their mere utterance under certain conditions of felicity. This is a deep insight so far as it goes. But its implications for personhood have yet to be identified.

To examine these implications, let us return to the logic of the gift, in particular the force (or *hau*), which Mauss saw, generalizing the Maori concept, as a quality that links the gift, the giver, and the recipient in such a manner as to compel the receiver to make a countergift or a further gift, thus revealing a logic of reciprocity that precedes even the initial gift. Mauss saw *hau* as a quality, which somehow linked the gift and the giver in a manner that compelled the countergift. We know that for Mauss this logic accounted for why gifts produced the obligation to return, after an interval of time that could not be reduced to a rule, a formula, or a legal contract. This interval of time is what allowed Pierre Bourdieu (1976) to posit the noneconomistic character of gift exchange and allowed Derrida (1992) to shift the entire focus of the gift away from exchange to the gift of time itself.

This mysterious force that binds gift to both giver and receiver was not further explored by anthropologists because it was not recognized that the gift here is an instance of the attachment of the dividual character of the giver to be attached to the gift and to spark a further tie to some dividual element of the receiver. Put another way, gifts and other objectified instruments in the ritual process do not create ties between "whole" individuals but rather between dividuals, who are in effect partial, volatile, and particular sorts of agents, capable of joining other dividuals in their capacity as kinsmen, traders, enemies, affines, ancestors, or descendants, all more like what we would today call roles rather than individuals. But the idea of role is itself so deeply anchored in the idea of a prior substrate or ground that we think of as the individual, that it does not capture the ontology of a dividualized society, since dividuals are, in such societies, the elementary constituents of individuals (and of other larger social aggregations) rather than mere aspects, dimensions, or "personae" of a foundational individual. This ontological reversal is the very definition of the dividual.

Just as the power of the gift may be seen to lie in the capacity of dividuals to create assemblages between themselves and others by combining with things (the gifts as such), so all ritual processes as described by anthropologists from van Gennep to Clifford Geertz may be reinterpreted as the metaphoric and metonymic techniques through which dividuals enter into dynamic and volatile assemblages. It is because the key actors (or actants) in ritually organized societies are dividuals, rather than individuals, that these rituals are capable of acquiring retroperformative force. If named and stable individuals were the subjects of such ritual processes, their assemblage into desirable configurations would have no more than the force of ratification or recognition of established logics of role, status, and norm. In ritually organized societies, since ritual is about the co-staging of uncertainty and certainty to handle volatility (in society, nature, and cosmos), retro-performativity benefits from the dynamic assemblage of dividuals, does not rely on the routinized confirmation of relations among individuals, as in own societies of contract. The volatility of interactions among dividuals requires some form of retro-performativity because totalities (wholes) can only be retro-engineered in a world composed of dividuals (parts).[6]

The Derivative and the Dividual

It remains now to link up the world of the financial derivative (embodying, as I have earlier suggested, a predatory logic of dividuation) to a more expansive view of the precapitalist ritual milieu, so as to open the door to a more radical, progressive and socially generative view of finance, wealth and risk. The best route to this argument is the recent work of Elie Ayache (2010). In chapters 5 and 6, I have referred to his major claim, which is that we have all been misled by the fact that prices are expressed in numbers, to believe that these numbers belong to temporal sets that are susceptible to probabilistic understanding.

Ayache is at pains to argue that the market, so far as financial tools are concerned, is not a reflective or post hoc process for aggregating, mediating, or commensurating buyers and sellers (or demand and supply). Rather, it is a creative force, an ontological absolute that precedes and is the condition of all pricing. Ayache does not refer to Durkheim, but his argument may be seen as a radical version of Durkheim's view on the prior ontological reality of society, in his famous argument in *The Elementary Forms of the Religious Life* (1995), about the social basis of the category of the sacred.

When we combine Ayache's view of the trading event with his account of the body of the trader and of the importance of writing as the key tool for the making of contingent claims (see chapter 6), we can see the possibilities for a deep convergence between Durkheim's ideas about collective effervescence and Ayache's idea of the trading event as the real site of market-making through agreements about price. The deep link here is between the trading floor or space (even when it is virtual or machine-mediated) and those of the moment of collective effervescence in the ritual life of Australian aboriginal societies. The shared element is the electricity, the metasocial sensation of belonging, and the deep identifications (body-to-body), which attend the creation of society in ritual (for Durkheim).

Still, a major puzzle remains about both the logic of the derivative and the logic of precapitalist ritual and this is where the idea of the dividual can come to our assistance. Recall that Durkheim, and his numerous followers (including Mauss, Lévi-Strauss, and Bourdieu, as well as numerous other anthropologists of the twentieth century), did not really unsettle the category of the individual as the foundational element of all social interaction and social institutions. In this sense Durkheim did not move away from Kant, with whose ideas about the origins of our primary categories (such as space and time) he took radical issue. It was not until the path-breaking work of Louis Dumont, in *Homo Hierarchicus* (1970) and a series of other books and essays, that the post-Renaissance idea of the individual was put into sharp comparative relief. But even Dumont contrasted Western individualism with Indic "holism," and did not really consider the idea of dividuality. This was the accomplishment of Marriott (1976) and, later, Marilyn Strathern (1988), as I have already argued. And these latter thinkers had, alas, little interest in the problem of performativity (even less in the issue of retro-performativity).[7]

If we now insert the idea of the dividual back into our reading of Durkheim, bearing in mind the link to Ayache's argument about derivative trading and its own logic of "backwardation" or retro-performativity, we can supply an answer to the peculiar way in which precapitalist societies invented a major modality for dealing with the uncertainty as the core predicament of human societies. *Rituals take their effect by the retro-performative creation of wholes out of parts, but the parts in question are dividuals, not individuals.* The reason that all rituals, however routinized, always carry an element of anxiety is that every ritual performance undertakes, as if for the first and last time, the effort to produce "wholes," such as individuals, clans, tribes, as well as affines, agnates, allies, and friends, out of inherently unstable, volatile, and contingent elements, namely dividuals. The momentary creation of "totalities," at any and all of these levels, is subject both to situational uncertainty (Will a counterparty be found to any ritual invitation? Will the gift be returned? Will the adolescent survive the wounds of the rite of passage? Will the new child be appropriately healthy? Will the crops actually grow?), as well as to a more primary uncertainty, which is whether the constituent dividual actors in any ritual scene, in any moment of collective effervescence, will stay stable enough to lend retrospective stability to an inherently volatile and contingent assemblage of dividuals.

In the case of market-making in derivatives, as described by Ayache, this volatility, contingency, and unpredictability are wrapped into the derivative instrument itself, and are a product of the slicing, dicing, and recombination that lies at the heart of the derivative form itself. *In both cases, the great accomplishment of backwardation (in the case of derivative trading) or retro-performativity (in the case of ritual performance) is to create options and hedges in and through the same sequence of actions.*[8] The option aspect of the event is its taking of the risk that some sort of whole can be created, even if temporarily, by the strategic assemblage of parts. The hedge aspect of the event is the reliance on some sort of routinized assumption that the larger model (of cosmological or market fundamentals) will guard against the inherent instability of the dividuals involved in the assemblage.

But there is also a critical difference between the ritual order and the market order. In the case of the ritual order, the dividuals entering into a performance are the *permanent* elements of the order, who take the temporary risk of assembling themselves into wholes (whether individual or corporate). In the case of the financialized order, the dividuals are *temporary* products of predatory dividuation (ranking, scoring, enumeration, quantification, monetization) who are put at risk by actors (brokers, traders, managers, analysts) who reserve the right to behave as individuals *in their own interest*. In short, in the ritual order all actors take the risk of entering into a risky assemblage, whereas in the financial order the risk is asymmetrically distributed between professional risk-takers (traders) at the expense of already dividuated actors who largely bear the downside risks of the market. This is the difference that is captured in the idea of predatory dividuation.

The Political Future

We are now in a position to raise the main political question that follows from this argument about dividuals, ritual, and derivative trading, which is: is there a way to transform the derivatives markets (and by extension the contemporary financial markets) into sites of progressive or democratic dividuation rather than sites of the current exploitative, asymmetric and antidemocratic financial order? In other words, can we leverage our argument about the dividual into a basis for a democratic politics of finance?

To answer this question an approach can partly be indicated here. The only way to convert the dividual into a genuinely empowered subject in today's predatory financial context is not by any form of return to a nonmonetized, nonfinancialized order, or any "refusal" of our current forms of debt and wealth creation, both of which imply a reversal of history that is both unrealistic and undesirable. What is called for is a radical change in the architecture of our social thought.

What we need to do is to rethink our primary vocabulary for social consociation so as to reflect the irreversible effects of financialized dividuation. For us, as social scientists, this will mean a radical reconstruction of such categories as group, class, mass, crowd, and multitude, as well as qualitative terms such as "public," "collective," "free," and "social." These two sets of concepts, which provide the armature of much of our current social theory, will need rebuilding with the assumption being that the elementary building blocks of the social are not individuals but dividuals, the latter being a much more unstable, volatile, contingent, and open element than the canonic individual that has so far anchored our social thought.

If we are able to undertake this thoroughgoing reform of our basic social vocabulary, we might be able to take such phenomena as spreads, volatility, liquidity, and risk, currently used to disenfranchise most dividuals, and imagine new forms of collective risk-taking through which the derivative will more closely approximate what Guy Debord called the "derive" (2007), that is, the practice of playful travel through urban landscapes that opens up the terrain of chance and serves as an antidote to the deadening routinization of everyday experience in late capitalism.[9]

In simpler terms, a radical social theory built on a contemporary definition of the dividual has the potential for reintroducing the play of chance into our social lives in a manner that allows *all of us* to engage in the risk-taking possibilities for creating wealth, rather than reserving this privilege to the 1 percent who reap the rewards of risk-taking, with the rest of us consigned to the status of risk-bearers and collective losers. This radical potential takes the derivative form to be a genuine instrument for the production of wealth in the present by taking risks on the future. But it also requires us to see ourselves as partial, contingent, and volatile beings who can leverage and resocialize our dividuality by exploiting the deep logic of the derivative form. This proposal is taken up again the next chapter.

Concluding by Example

To imagine the political implications of the argument about the contrastive relationship between dividual and individual in capitalist and ritual-based societies, I turn to a brief analysis of the housing market in Mumbai, where an activist movement of slum dwellers has been struggling to establish rights to housing for homeless of underhoused slum communities for more than three decades.

I have written extensively about the ritual, social, and political life of this movement in a recent book (Appadurai 2013). In the present context, what is striking is how dividuality expresses itself in a context where a population of about 6 million persons lacks legitimate access to housing and where, as a consequence, financial markets, mortgages, and derivatives are essentially absent. At the same time Mumbai, with a growing population of more than 16 million persons, is a financial and corporate hub for India, which has a highly active stock market, many insurance companies, and a number of national and global financial firms (banks, hedge funds, and nonformal lending institutions). The products and services offered by these financial players directly affect the housing development market in Mumbai, as well as the lives of numerous members of Mumbai's middle classes who participate in banking, borrowing, stock investments, mortgages, and insurance. This financial market is in the process of developing and is only gradually becoming rationalized in the manner of its Western counterparts, in regards to regulation, risk, law, and data gathering.

In this respect, cities like Mumbai and societies like India occupy an intermediate and transitional space between the ritualized societies which I have been discussing in this chapter and the advanced financial economies of the West. As a result, Mumbai (and India) also exhibit some dynamic contrasts and connections between the ritualized dividuation of small-scale, low-technology societies and the financialized dividuation of the contemporary West.

The slum activists with whom I worked in Mumbai are keenly aware of the dangers of the fully financialized environment in which they increasingly function, in a city whose square-foot real estate prices rival those of New York, London, and Tokyo. They are surrounded by developers who would transform slum areas into high-rise towers and middle-class housing, bankers who would like to draw them into the micro-savings markets and politicians who would like to use them as vote banks.

These slum communities, led by an alliance of activists, can be regarded as pursuing a progressive brand of dividualism, albeit in a powerful capitalist environment. This characterization is based on several observations. First, the slum dwellers I spoke to always expressed a strong ideology of anti-individualism, based on their sense that individualism was closely linked to selfishness, greed, and antisocial tendencies, which could be expressed in the behavior of members regarding money, personal possessions, or temporary housing. At the same time, they expressed strong aversion to descriptions of their collective identity in terms of class, interest group, party, or faction, all of which they regarded as misleading ways of talking about their sense of community. This resistance always puzzled me until recently, when I began to look at my decade-long experience with them in terms of the broader and deeper Indic idea of dividual actors and actions, as shown by McKim Marriott and many of his students. I have already discussed the key features of the idea of the dividual but the relevance of this idea to Mumbai's slum dwellers needs further elaboration.

The slum dwellers of Mumbai are not a classical anthropological community. But they are all Indian and do come from a variety of linguistic, ethnic, and caste groups that have deep Indian roots. In this regard, they do share certain Indic ideas about health, wealth, and sociality. In Mumbai they may be regarded as a quasi-caste, because they share a situation into which they were mostly born, their destinies look fairly predetermined, and they are regarded as a biophysical category by other urban citizens, in often thinly biologized ideas about slum morality, hygiene, and disease. They react to this biologization by regarding themselves, to some extent, as a natural group, with common interests, obligations, and moralities. Poverty and slum dwelling have thus become partly accommodated to the lens of caste morality and ideology.

Part of this morality is the idea that moral agency is unstable, relational, and situational. At the same time such identities are regarded as rooted in some sort of natural, biophysical, and organic order. The primary insight of Marriott's ideas about the radical difference between Indian and Western moral cosmologies was that the Indian ones do not recognize a sharp line between mind and body, self and other, nature and culture, law and predisposition. Marriott called this point of view monistic (or nondualistic). While it might seem a long journey from Indic cosmological ideas to the political practices of the Mumbai slum dwellers, the connection is real. Its most clear expression is the refusal of these slum dwellers to allow themselves to be defined as individuals, in the common modern sense, and to insist on their collective identity. This in itself might be viewed as a conventional modern form of social solidarity, as expressed in the language of class, party, income group, or interest group. But the sense of collective identity among these slum dwellers is more radically attuned to the dynamic linkages between bodies, infrastructure, technical assemblages, and situational instability and is in fact expressive of a dividual cosmology.

This can most clearly be seen in their understanding of the importance of toilets and defecation in the struggle for rights for slum communities. I have written elsewhere (Appadurai 2001) of the ways in which toilet festivals (*sandas mela*) have been a key strategy of this urban movement to redefine defecation, sanitation, and sociality in the Mumbai context, as well as in many other locations in urban India where they work. The problem of toilets is a vital part of the politics of urban poverty throughout the world, and in India it bears the additional burden of highly valued notions of purity, pollution, stigma, and degradation, as evidenced in the powerful social bias against those Untouchables who historically served as scavengers, toilet-cleaners, and night soil carriers both in rural and urban India. The toilet politics of the Mumbai slum dwellers have made community toilets, designed, built, and operated by the slum communities themselves a site of empowerment and dignity rather than of exclusion and pollution. They have done this by making toilets more like community centers (in which the person charged with maintaining a new toilet block lives in a small unit above the community toilet) and have invited government officials and other political figures to launch these community toilets in much the manner that the inauguration of temples and deities in much of India is done, with flowers, coconuts, and public celebrations accompanying these events. This is part of a complex strategy to make defecation a publically recognized and valid platform for social dignity, in an environment where defecation in public is always a sign of radical dispossession, especially in urban India.

Behind this reclamation of toilets from being a site of deficit, disease, and degradation, there lies a complex view of how best bodies, bodily wastes, sociality, and community can be reassembled in situations where space, access to infrastructure, and privacy are always scarce. It requires a view of slum communities as formed of dividuals whose shared bodily practices are grounded in the capacity of such groups to recombine traditional Indian social categories. Here it is important to note that these slum communities come from diverse castes, ethnic groups, and religious communities throughout India, each of which would traditionally have placed great emphasis on their differences from one another, however minute. By redesigning and revalorizing community toilets, these communities create a radical bodily space in which a derivative and dividual logic is turned to the project of finding positive value (solidarity) where only negative value (shit) previously existed. This transformative and derivative operation can only occur in an environment where dividuals are always in an unstable, volatile, and relational environment of social and moral reproduction. To place toilets and sanitation at the center of a politics of "deep democracy" (Appadurai 2001) literally turns classic Indic dividualism on its head, and turns shit into social value and exclusion into empowerment.

This is thus a fascinating glimpse of a progressive politics of dividualism, equally distinct from modern Western possessive individualism and from classical Hindu dividualism, which has a powerful conservative thrust, insofar as it locks castes and other social categories into a persistent form of inequality. The Mumbai slum dwellers have assembled a different, and derivative, form of dividuality that may properly be called political and progressive in that it embodies an immanent critique both of classical Hindu thought as well as of the financialized individualism that surrounds them in modern Mumbai.

This instance is not likely to stand alone, either in India or in the rest of the world. I point to a possible third way for the politics of the dividual and the derivative to be reassembled in the interests of social justice. For if shit can be turned to positive value by a group on the margins of predatory capitalism in a city like Mumbai, surely other forms of labor, energy, and value can be similarly reclaimed for progressive and dividualized forms of social wealth, which are derivative in form but socially inclusive and expansive in spirit.

CHAPTER EIGHT

THE GLOBAL AMBITIONS
OF FINANCE

Introduction

Capitalism today surrounds and saturates us in a way it never did before. In its home regions, notably in the United States, it has taken the form of deep financialization. The volume and value of financial transactions now vastly exceed the value of industrial goods and services. Since the early 1970s we have had the rapid development of a host of financial instruments that were barely imaginable in the time of Karl Marx. The breakthrough that made this financial explosion possible was the idea that risk itself could be monetized, allowing a small set of actors to take risks on risks. This is the core of the logic of the derivative, an instrument that has allowed financial technicians and managers to make virtually every part of our everyday lives susceptible to monetization. In this way, as we have seen, housing has now been turned into a machine for monetizing mortgages; the environment has been monetized through carbon trading and many other derivatives; education has been captured through sophisticated methods of creating student debt; health and insurance have been thoroughly penetrated by models of risk, arbitrage, and bets on the future. In short, everyday life is linked to capital not so much by the mechanism of the surplus value of labor but by making us all risk-bearers, whose aggregate risk can be endlessly combined and recombined to provide new forms of risk-taking and profit-making by the financial industries. We are all laborers now, regardless of what we do, insofar as our primary reason for being is to enter into debt through being forced to monetize the risks of health, security, education, housing, and much else in our lives.[1]

This situation is most visible in the advanced capitalist countries and hence the financial collapse of 2007–8 was primarily felt and amplified in these very countries. But very few countries in the world escaped the effects of the collapse, since finance capital had been spreading its activities worldwide for at least the last thirty years. Still, many parts of the Global South did not experience the shock of the collapse as profoundly as did the United States and Europe. This measure of insulation was possible primarily because the new derivative logics, creating multiple loops between debt, risk, and speculation, were less advanced in these countries. Another way to put it is that in the countries of the Global South, the process by which all debt is made potentially monetizable, through derivative instruments, has been less rapid and more uneven than it has been in the countries of the North Atlantic.

However, the global spread of the financial imaginary has by no means been arrested or compromised. Banks, hedge funds, and insurance companies are aggressively pushing their way into new markets, lobbying for legislation that will bring the same untrammeled debt markets from which they profited (and which also crashed in 2008) to the countries of the Global South. Thus, it is only a matter of time before the countries of the Global South also find themselves fully exposed to the volatility, inscrutability, and extra-legality of the derivative-based financial markets of the North. As James Baldwin once said in another context, "no more water, the fire next time" (1963).

How can we resist the sense that this global process is inevitable and that it cannot be subverted? A further question is: what sort of politics needs to be produced to resist it? The main answer that has emerged in various parts of the world is debt-refusal, as in important segments of the Occupy movement. Debt refusal by mortgage owners, students, pension-holders, and others is certainly a legitimate political tactic, insofar as it offers an immediate tool for starving the beast of financial capitalism. But is it enough? Is it even the best way of making capitalism work for the 99 percent?

In this book, I have aimed to develop a different view of financial capitalism, one that does not see the logic of the derivative as inherently inequitable or evil. My strategy was built on a return to Weber and Durkheim, but through a financial lens, and through Weber's eyes especially, to engage Marx. Marx's central insight about the workings of industrial capitalism was (in *Capital* [1992]) to notice the distinction between absolute and relative surplus value. In simple terms, absolute surplus value was to be found in increasing the amount of labor that a firm could apply to producing commodities for sale, as by increasing the number of workers or by increasing the length of the workday. Relative surplus value, on the other hand, was generated by improvements in technology, workplace organization, or other means by which labor productivity could be increased without hiring more workers or paying for more labor time. This is how a given firm could compete with other firms producing the same commodity. The key to the appropriation of relative surplus value was to make a given amount of labor produce more profit, without increasing wages. The difference was profit in the hands of the capitalist.

Today's financial capitalism, which Marx could not have entirely foreseen in his day, does not primarily work through the making of profit in the commodity sphere, though a certain part of the capitalist economy still operates in this sphere. By far the larger portion works by making profit on the monetization of risk, and risk is made available to the financial markets through debt in its myriad forms. All of us who live in a financialized economy generate debt in many forms: consumer debt, housing debt, health debt, and others related to these. Capitalist forms also operate through debt, since borrowing on the capital markets has become much more important than issuing stock or equity.

From this point of view, the major form of labor today is not labor for wages but rather labor for the production of debt. Some of us today are no doubt wage-laborers, in the classic sense. But many of us are in fact debt-laborers, whose main task is to produce debt that can then be further monetized for profit by financial entrepreneurs who control the means of the production of profit through monetizing debts. The main vehicle for this form of profit-making is the derivative, and thus throughout this book I have tried to show that the derivative is the central means by which relative surplus value is produced in a financialized economy.

From this it follows that the key to transforming the current form of financial capitalism is to *seize and appropriate the means of the production of debt*, in the interest of the vast class of debt producers, rather than the small class of debt-manipulators. From this point of view, it is not debt as such that is bad, since it allows us to bring future value into the present, and to create far greater quantities of wealth than we had ever imagined. The challenge, rather, is to socialize and democratize the profit produced by monetization of debt so that those of us who actually produce debt can also be the main beneficiaries of its monetization.

Back to Ritual, Forward to Black-Scholes

I have argued in the preceding chapters of this book that Weber and Durkheim offer us an understanding of the co-presence of uncertainty and certainty in ritualized social orders (e.g., religious or magical). The central problem of financial practice in the domain of derivatives is the problem of arriving at options pricing in real-time trades, given that the available models for options pricing (even the Black-Scholes model and all its elaborations) do not offer unambiguous predictions about options prices. Several major theorists (Ayache 2010; Derman 2011; MacKenzie 2006) seem to be struggling for a language to describe the ways in which the social enters into trading decisions when the models provide no decisive guidance. I have suggested in earlier chapters that a rereading of Weber and Durkheim from the point of view of this gap in current theories of derivatives trading offers a richer and fuller way of grasping how the social enters into trading practice. I have also tried to show that the joint deployment of some ideas of Weber and Durkheim on what we might call ritual practice "under conditions of uncertainty" can provide a bridge into how traders make the leap from the space of probability (quantifiable) to the space of uncertainty (unquantifiable).

The relationship of cosmology (the model) to ritual (the actual activity of trading) is not symmetrical. Ritual practice is an effort to recalibrate the world (as it exists) so as to achieve a closer relationship to the cosmos (ideally a relationship of identity); financial practice is an effort to use the model to recalibrate the actually existing world so as to generate riskless return. This relationship of symmetry and inversion between the worlds of ritual and of trading comes into play because of the role of the *interval* (timing and duration between the present and any specific future date) and the peculiar nature of *retro-performativity* in the ritual and financial spheres.

This approach enables us to describe how the relatively arcane theories and practices of the derivative trading world actually colonize large parts of our life worlds through mechanisms of reverberation, amplification, and potential saturation. In an older Habermasian idiom, we might say that we are now close to describing ways in which a specific part of the system-world captures large parts of the life-world since the 1970s. The idea of reverberation or amplification allows us to see finance not as an engine or cause of the wider effects of risk-based thinking but simply as one site among many, which nonetheless exposes the logic of the derivative most clearly.

Both ritual and finance constitute specialized worlds whose technical practices are designed equally to anchor and to manage profane or everyday moments, problems, and dilemmas, especially those that have the qualities of risk and uncertainty. Each does so by directly manipulating key parts of a general cosmology, whose internal structure is imaged on the market (in the case of finance) and on society (in the case of noncapitalist ritual). Both these latter abstractions have the dual quality of being presupposed by the technical practices of traders and ritual practitioners, and of bringing these abstractions into being through practice in the here-and-now of the ritual or trading process. In both cases, there is a surrounding environment of narrative that also assures a steady fortification of conviction about the abstractions of society and market, in one case through practices of myth, story-telling, and folkloric forms (such as proverbs and dream narratives) and in the other case through business news, education, and other forms of capitalist reportage.

In the case of ritual practice (seen by many anthropologists as more or less the same as magic), a line of thought going back from Malinowski to Stanley Tambiah via Evans-Pritchard and J. L. Austin has identified some key ways in which words acquire magical power, rituals effect action at a distance, and magical actions work through the same mechanisms as performative speech acts (more exactly through illocution and perlocution). Benjamin Lee and Edward LiPuma have shown how this performative dimension also works through retro-performativity, that is, by engineering presuppositions by enacting illocutions. A loose way to put a great deal of what this tradition of thought has discovered is the insight that the combination of metonym and metaphor lies at the heart of the ritual. That is, any sequence of ritual action acquires its reverberative, amplificatory, and rippling effect on ordinary life by building on a series of links between things that resemble one another and things that are actually connected (as parts, components, or extensions) to one another.

It is this "dynamic replication" through metaphor and metonym that may be the most important way in which finance also achieves its amplificatory effects. Let us examine this claim more closely. Finance clearly has achieved a part of its dominant role in the contemporary economy by a series of metaphorical claims about the resemblance between how money can make money and the dynamics of monetization in other areas of life. The core or anchoring metaphor here is the metaphor of risk itself. There has been a major breakthrough in the social sciences that has analyzed the ways in which we have become a "risk society," in the phrase of Ulrich Beck (1992), that is, a society dominated by probabilistic, actuarial, and computational approaches to uncertainty in every area of social life. What has not been observed is that this colonizing process is in fact predicated on the risk metaphor as a way of handling uncertainty in every area of life. This saturation of all of our lives by the risk metaphor precedes and anchors the actual operations of risk algorithms and risk expertise in such areas as health, housing, and education. This extension of the risk metaphor to much of the rest of social life is accompanied by the spread of a series of related and interconnected metaphors, of which the key ones are the spread, hedging, liquidity, and volatility, with a related series being less widespread but also relevant.

The journey of metaphors from one area of life to another is hardly new or interesting. There have been endless analyses of sports metaphors, war metaphors, and market metaphors as they crisscross to describe other aspects of social life. The interesting dynamic is when metaphors begin to be hitched to metonyms, so as to produce materialization, reverberation, and amplification. In the ritual world, as I have noted already, this largely happens through the dissemination of key cosmological ideas through various forms of narrative, and so it is in the financial world. In addition, however, there is also the key role of metonym in stitching together ever-widening metaphoric distances. This latter metonymic dynamic has yet to be fully understood.

In this respect, Clifford Geertz's brilliant essay on the cockfight (1972) offers us perhaps the richest example of how the ritual frame is metonymically stitched to the wide social frame by putting status hierarchies at risk through the deep play of bets during the cockfight, thus making the metaphor of the "cock" dynamic and making it reverberate into profane life. What Geertz shows us, through the internal dynamic of the relationship between the center bets and the side bets, is a microcosm of the wider dynamic rippling that links the ritual sphere to all of social life. Neither metaphor nor metonym can succeed in producing this rippling on its own. It is their combined workings that produce the larger effect.

So how can we apply this understanding of metaphor and metonym to the wider reverberations of financial models and practices in contemporary social life? To do this, we need to look closely at the ways in which the key terms that constitute the inner dynamics of trading (such as volatility, hedging, spreads, options, and futures) operate both as metaphors and as metonyms in contemporary life. Here the logic of the derivative is crucial—and even more, its language, in the promissory, performative sense that I have elaborated throughout this book. Yet, to understand how and to what extent this financial logic and its material forms are spreading in other parts of the world, we need to make a detour, and pay attention to the current ways in which finance as an expert discipline (taught in business schools and practiced by bankers, traders, investors, and shareholders) has broken free of the shackles of its mother discipline—economics—even this secession has yet to be publically acknowledged.

A Star Is Born

I have long been curious about the birth and death of disciplines. We know that the disciplines, as organized and professionalized fields of expertise, are modern inventions, and most scholars have always recognized the historicity of their fields. In our own area of interest, the human economy, we have come a long way from Aristotle's vision of the norms of the household to today's sense of economics, as a field that models, theorizes, predicts, and measures the varieties of human efforts to manage scarcity and govern the distribution of material goods.

We also know that economics has established itself in the twentieth century as the dominant social science, largely through its appeal to states and to markets, since it has succeeded in promoting itself as the principal explicator of the latter to the former. Such outstanding scholar as Albert Hirschman, Timothy Mitchell, and Keith Hart have told us important parts of the story of the imperial march of economics, which, especially in its radical American versions, purports to explain everything from sports and the drug trade to wars and famines with its elegant tool kit.

Yet, unnoticed by most of us, a new Trojan has emerged from the horse of economics. This is the field of finance, originally housed in business schools as a poor cousin of economics departments but today increasingly mindless of its progenitor and proud to proclaim its dominion over states, hedge funds, stock exchanges, pension funds, mortgage markets, insurance companies, and through them over much of the terrain of ordinary life. Parts of this story have already been told with insight by such scholars as Randy Martin (2002) and Donald MacKenzie (2006), but no one has as yet observed the growing declaration of independence from economics by practitioners of finance studies, something that amounts to a worldwide disciplinary decolonization that is not an entirely benign development.

The public information on academic websites, university admissions documents, and professional disciplinary websites is scrupulously polite on both sides of the economics/finance divide. The subtext, especially from the economics side, is always about how economics is more "theoretical" and finance is more "applied." But the real tensions are older and deeper.

Even at a university such as the University of Chicago, where much of modern finance was born, the inequality between economics and finance was palpable. Here, in the heart of the neoliberal theory machine, in spite of the friendly relationships between Milton Friedman, Merton Miller, Eugene Fama, and others on both sides of the divide, there was no doubt that the driving heart of theory was in the economics department, and that the big finance thinkers were, at best, smart engineers.

To this day, there is no public disclosure about the lowly status of finance as a field of study in the eyes of economists. But there is a lot of rumbling in the jungle. The best evidence, though it was not intended to be used in this manner, comes from the excellent 2006 book by Donald MacKenzie, called *An Engine Not a Camera*, a sober account of the rise of finance as a distinct field, dateable to the early 1970s, with precursory signals going back much earlier.

What this careful historical account of the rise of finance, as a field distinct from economics, does is to show us the key thinkers, models, and problems that allow finance to claim today that it is a field with a pedigree, a canon, a method, and subject matter of its own. Because MacKenzie is remarkably even-handed and nonpartisan, his work commands attention. To draw out the key pieces of the evidence, they are as follows.

The first step is the development of finance as a form of engineering or of calculation, simply directed to valuing assets, both for purposes of accounting in the life of firms, and as an aspect of the problem of pricing, especially for money assets, in which markets can either be new, nonexistent, or highly volatile. The best examples of such assets, of course, are options and futures, of which the most developed contemporary forms are derivatives in their myriad forms. One might say the birth of finance as a separate discipline lies in the moment when the pricing of assets becomes more important than the pricing of primary commodities or, more precisely, when contracts surrounding assets become more important than primary contract prices. To put it even more simply, prices in the world of derivatives are in effect not so much prices as they are contracts about prices, as Elie Ayache (2010) makes evident in his brilliant account of the limits of probabilistic thinking in the world of derivative trading. One might even go one step further and say that the intellectual independence of finance lies in the prices of contracts rather than in contracts about price, which lie at the heart of neoclassical economics.

There is a second way in which finance established its freedom from neoclassical economics and that is in regard to the work of Frank Knight, notably his classic essay on risk and uncertainty. Knight, as I have already noted in chapters 2 and 3, was immensely indebted to Weber and was pursuing a line of thought that sought to place the uncertainty faced by the entrepreneur at the heart of modern economics, just as his contemporary, Schumpeter, coming out of a different strand of the Austrian economic tradition, focused on the role of innovation in capitalist organizations. Finance completely eliminates Knightian uncertainty (the unquantifiable unknown) from its purview and builds an entire science on the foundations of risk (the quantifiable unknown), primarily by the refinement of probability-based statistics. It is this probabilistic foundation that has been pushed to its extreme by Nassim Taleb and now put into question by Elie Ayache (2010), who argues, using the work of Alain Badiou and Quentin Meillasoux, that contingency and not probability is the key to the logic of the derivative, and that written contracts and not probabilistically predictable prices are the key to derivative trading. For our purposes here, it is not these latter arguments that are crucial, so much as the elimination of nonnumerical uncertainty from the Knightian heritage by the theorists of high finance, notably Black and Scholes, whose 1973 model for the pricing of options remains the Bible and the black box of all options price modeling.

The elimination of nonnumerical or qualitative uncertainty from the space of financial modeling is radical, for it also eliminates the entire tradition of possibilities that begins with Max Weber and opens up the question of the spirit, the ethos and the habitus of profit-making behavior, apart from its algorithmic aspects. This is the line of thinking that was being explored by Weber, and later by Knight and Schumpeter, and is the heart of the argument I have developed throughout this book about the ethos of qualitative uncertainty, and specifically of the derivative sensibility, by reopening the relevance not just of Weber, but also of Durkheim, Bourdieu, Goffman, Geertz, and other nonorthodox thinkers interested in the calculative habitus and its underling cultural dispositions. My own effort to reopen the dialogue between Weber, Durkheim, and some aspects of Marx belongs to and is informed by this collective dialogue. Among other things, therefore, this book can be read as an effort to simultaneously endorse the escape of finance studies from the crippling cage of neoclassical economics and to open up an alternative history that could re-engage the great earlier traditions of political economy while doing a coronary bypass around the last century of neoclassical hegemony. This exercise has various implications but the one I pursue in the remainder of this chapter is the way in which this new ideology of finance—largely set free of neoclassical economics—is also the key to the global journey of financial instruments and markets, and to the uneven ways in which the world beyond Europe and the United States is taking up the seductions of finance—as a discipline, an ideology, and a technology for monetizing risk and thus creating hitherto unimaginable scales of wealth.

One way to get a sense of the globalization of finance is by looking closely at the journey of one specific derivative instrument—the credit default swap (CDS)—to show how CDS instruments were the critical, efficient cause of the housing mortgage collapse in 2007–8 in the United States and were widely characterized in just those terms. Bankers, investors, and policymakers in societies as diverse as France, Japan, Brazil, South Africa, and India noticed the danger of CDS as a way to increase liquidity in financial markets and create new wealth. Yet these forms are rapidly entering these places and more, as financial institutions, like moths drawn to the flame, sacrifice prudence for these new instruments for profit-making. The entry of CDS instruments into economies that had very little interest in volatile markets, risky investments of national wealth, and outsize bond markets is the first step toward the untrammeled growth of the CDS form.

Credit default swaps, put in the simplest terms, resemble insurance of the ordinary sort, in which we protect ourselves against adverse events in which we have a direct stake, such as illness, property loss, or various forms of catastrophe. Credit default swaps, however, have a special quality in which two parties are able to make a derivative contract involving a third party—a company, a bank, a country, or a pooled set of mortgages (itself a derivative bundle), in the event that there is a default by this third party. What is especially risky about the CDS is that it is purely speculative and neither party in the contract has an investment in the underlying asset. It is an insurance bet freed from any form of ownership in the underlying asset.

Since the CDS is all about credit, it is a derivative, which operates only in large and volatile bond markets, rather than in material commodities. In short it is a bet on *the risk of a defaulting debt*. This peculiar market in which credit is another word for debt (corporate, personal, or national) is premised on the outsized growth of the bond market, which is all about the borrowing of huge sums to finance current expenses by large institutions. Bonds on their own are not especially risky, but once they get sliced, diced, bundled, and securitized so they can be traded for their future value, which is independent of the value of the underlying asset, they become the keys to *leverage*, another distinctive feature of our era of financialization, in which I can use my current assets (which may themselves be speculative or unrealized) to borrow even larger sums. The bond market in the United States today is worth roughly $38 trillion, which is about twice the total value of the stock market.[2] Put more simply, taking risk on the future of debt is worth far more than taking risk on the value of a company or product in the future, through the buying and selling of stocks.

Credit default swaps can be based on any underlying commodity but it is in the housing market that they achieved their biggest prominence and thus became a critical part of the subprime mortgage crisis of 2007–8. The difference between the role of the CDS in the housing market and in regard to other assets is that housing is the area that most directly links ordinary, often vulnerable homeowners to the most exotic financial instruments. The fact that the CDS market was a crucial element of the 2007–8 in the world's most sophisticated financial market did not go unnoticed by central bankers and policymakers throughout the world. But few have been able to resist the temptation to enter the bond market in a big way, to open the door to the derivative market as its main current expression, and thus to consider enabling trading in the CDS market, in spite of the ugly lessons from 2007–8. This global seduction by dangerous financial instruments is what I turn to next, by looking at the CDS market in India.

India in the Derivative World

Before looking at how the Indian state is looking at derivatives in general and credit default swaps in particular, let us step back and consider the broader argument I have developed throughout this book. The central insight that I have tried to develop has to do with the nature of derivative contracts as promises, in the Austinian sense, which require certain conditions of felicity to function socially. I have proposed that the systemic failure of the derivatives market in 2007–8 was above all a failure of language and, more pointedly, of the burden of risk spread across a massive and interlinked system of promises that outgrew their conditions of felicity. Within the Euro-American context, blame was assigned to greedy investors, lax credit-ratings agencies, regulators asleep on the job, or sometimes simply the "wish" of the market to cleanse itself of greed, inefficiency, corruption, overregulation, or underregulation. No one thought to blame the linguistic and moral burden of creating a vast interlinked chain of promises that encouraged the total severance of reciprocal relations from rapid circulation and leveraged derivative assets.

India is an example of how the new financial order is entering the wider world, but it is no mere example with its population of 1.25 billion and a growing middle class almost the size of the entire population of the United States (current estimates set the number at 250 million persons, and growing rapidly). Also, India is perhaps the major site of the movement from a state-dominated quasi-socialist economy to a substantially liberalized economy, a process that began in the mid-1980s, well before the fall of the Berlin Wall. India has a complex, regionally based political system that has thrived on democratic elections since the early 1950s and has a vigorous free press and a strong and assertive judiciary. In many ways, India is a model democracy, except that it also has massive systemic corruption, a poor human rights record with minorities, and, most importantly, a large population that lives in abject poverty or near poverty that some estimate at a number close to 70 percent of its total population, which amounts to almost at least 800 million persons. It is also a country with a weak public health system, a massive Hindu nationalist movement that despises non-Hindu minorities, and a poor record of building infrastructure, which foreign investors (and their Indian counterparts) regularly decry, as well as having a massive military force that (barely) controls insurgencies in Kashmir, the North-East, and in the Maoist belt, which covers a wide swath of tribal and agricultural zones from Nepal to the deep south of India. So India is an exemplary democracy but not a model for anyone.

India has also had a sophisticated elite that has run its affairs from the time that it gained independence from the British to the present day. Over these six decades and more, India has produced some of the world's most distinguished economists, including the Nobel Prize–winning economist Amartya Sen. Today India's economists stand in disarray. The prime minister, Narendra Modi, swept in with a massive electoral victory for his Hindu nationalist party, the Bharatiya Janata Party (BJP), a few months ago, reflecting the worldwide trend toward global marketization combined with local cultural puritanism. Modi would like to turn up the dial on aggressive economic growth and corporate capitalism and turn back the clock on tolerance, pluralism, and secularism. He is between a rock and a hard place but he is unlikely to slow down the creep toward aggressive financialization in India. His economic advisors are unsure about how to engage the seductions of global finance.

The fact is that India, like most of the world today, is facing the escape of finance from economics and, as a consequence, is poorly positioned to manage the temptations of the new financial instruments. Since its independence, India's economy has been a mixture of socialist and capitalist models, with a substantial role for central planning but with a growing place for capitalist management, investment, and profit models. Beginning in 1985 India has seen a steady push for "reforms" from international organizations such as the IMF and the World Bank, its own capitalist class and a section of its own policymakers. "Reforms" typically mean deregulation of key industries, more foreign investment, and more incentives for capital to invest in Indian industries. The main institution that has had the challenge of balancing the demands of the global economic system and national priorities, such as infrastructure development, poverty reduction, and food self-sufficiency, is the Reserve Bank of India (RBI), the central bank of India. According to the preamble to its founding constitution, its purpose is "to regulate the issue of Bank Notes and keeping of reserves with a view to securing monetary stability in India and generally to operate the currency and credit system of the country to its advantage."[3]

This simple statement includes the key words "credit system," which puts the RBI in charge of all matters ranging from the overall national currency reserves, balance of trade, and banking system, and to all forms of loans, debts, and bonds, and financial devices that are legitimate in India. Today, it means that the RBI is the principal decision-maker about the growth of bond markets, of derivatives, and of household borrowing, including housing mortgages in India. Thus, though the RBI is run by economists specializing in monetary policy, it is primarily a financial institution, which, like the Fed in the United States, does not control the economy except through the control of monetary policy, fiscal regulations, and, above all, the major interest rates for commercial paper. The RBI works closely with the Finance Ministry, the state-controlled commercial banks, and all organizations concerned with the regulation of the stock and bond markets in India.

Like all central banks throughout the world, the RBI is charged with responsibility for liquidity in the Indian financial markets. Liquidity is the central idea of finance, while neoclassical economics takes liquidity as the default background for its models and theories. Both economists and finance professionals mean the same thing by liquidity, which is the relative speed and ease with which any asset (bond, a stock, a home, a company, or a complex derivative) can be converted to cash. A highly liquid financial environment is one in which most assets can be converted quickly and at a good price. A highly illiquid financial environment is one in which most assets have trouble being converted to cash quickly or without lowering their prices dramatically. The 2007–8 crisis was, from this point of view, a liquidity crisis, namely one in which financial assets became extremely hard to exchange for cash, until the

US government pumped huge amounts of cash into the lending institutions to "prime the pump." In one statement after another, before, during and after the financial meltdown of 2007–8, many major bankers adduced liquidity as the ultimate moral justification of the financial markets, as "God's work" in the widely cited words of Lloyd Blankfein, the chairman of Goldman Sachs.

Once we understand the logic of providing liquidity as the ethical foundation of the financial industries, it becomes possible to see that the justification of the growing variety, scale, and profitability of derivatives (including the CDS instruments that brought down the housing mortgage market) is as the most sophisticated tools for increasing liquidity in the financial markets. This liquidity, in turn, is seen as the basis of credit, investment, and growth and here "God's work" through finance meets the central tenet of neoclassical economics in this century, which is that growth is the key to market health, competitiveness, and efficiency. The invisible hand works best when it has more fingers. But for finance professionals their portion of God's work ends with the provision of liquidity. What banks, companies, and wealthy individuals with the liquidity at their disposal do is the work of another department of "God's work," which has to do with technology, efficient markets, and innovations in manufacturing and distribution. The latter are the business of economics, not of finance, at least not of finance in its most powerful and abstract forms.

In India, the God's work of derivatives was ushered in dramatically in June 2011, a full three years after CDS excesses in the mortgage market in the United States had brought the whole financial system close to total collapse. There was considerable excitement about this announcement from some parts of the finance community but others were cautious. The guidelines took some pains to set up ways in which the dangers of the CDS market in the United States that led up to the housing mortgage collapse could be forestalled. Among these was an effort to restrict this market to Indian citizens and, more important, to stipulate that no one without a direct interest in the underlying commodity that was being insured against default in a CDS could participate in this market. In effect, this made the CDS more like a conventional insurance transaction, in which bearers of the direct commodity risk (such as a home that risked fire or flood) could wager on the default of the insurance holder. There is evidence now that this rule is likely to be relaxed, thus opening the CDS market to third parties. In other words, parties A and B can make a credit default swap based on our estimations of the likelihood that party C will default. In the logic of derivatives seen as system of promises, as I have argued in chapter 1, this amounts to making a wager about a third party being unable to fulfill their promise to yet other remote parties.

Following this guideline from the RBI, the first major credit default swap was made by a major Indian bank, ICICI, with another bank, IDBI in regard to ICICI's loan to the Rural Electrification Corporation of India. This was followed by other CDS deals in India but the market is growing slower than expected, partly because of the RBI's restrictions that make it difficult to make CDS deals in a purely speculative spirit.

The small market in the CDS form in India is not likely to remain small since the housing market in India is growing steadily and there is a growing appetite for mortgages, which are then open to bundling, securitization, and further derivative-based speculation, as happened in the years prior to 2007 in the United States. This appetite can be seen in the rapidly growing market for small loans to poor people who have no credit history at all, not just poor credit histories. This Indian market has recently been opened to what are called nonbanking financial institutions, the most important of which are loan companies, some of which have recently grown large enough to enter the housing mortgage market, the stock exchanges, corporate philanthropy, and the growing field of microfinance, the making of small loans to India's large population of poor people who have essentially no collateral. This growing field in the Indian mortgage market is roughly parallel to the subprime mortgage market in the United States, which has been discussed in detail in earlier chapters of this book.

A simple way to summarize the Indian situation, in regard to mortgages, derivatives, and the risk of a speculative meltdown of the sort that occurred in 2007 and 2008, largely in more developed financial economies, is that two relevant processes are now in play that could spell serious trouble when they come into contact. One is the market in derivative instruments, such as credit default swaps that allow risky wagers to be made between financial players who have no interest in the "credit event" or default as an economic event in itself, because they have no stake in the underlying commodity, which is being insured against in the CDS. The second process is the growth of the housing mortgage market, in which bigger banks are committed to drawing the growing Indian middle classes, and the smaller banks and nonbanking financial institutions (i.e., dressed-up loan sharks) are drawing in India's loan-seeking poor, who have no credit history and very little collateral. Together these two segments amount to perhaps half a billion people, and it is impossible to imagine that the RBI will be able to resist the pressure of financial lobbies to draw this huge and growing world of debts into the derivatives market. When that happens, the linguistic fragility that characterizes the interlinked promises of the derivatives market will have the same potential for disaster as it showed in 2007–8.

I have focused on India up to this point because of my special interest in it. But it is evident that the worldwide market in derivatives is very hard to contain, regulate or resist. Countries as diverse as South Africa, Russia, Greece, and Brazil have already encountered (or created) serious risks associated with derivatives trading, and often the crises precipitated by derivatives in these countries involves major US banks, insurance companies, and private investors. Official supporters of the global derivatives industry and its most radical opponents, strangely enough, agree on the core of the danger of derivatives coming from the opacity of their legal structure (not their mathematics) and of the weakness of legal enforcement of the contractual provisions, which define the effectiveness of the derivative. In Russia, for example, the courts have had trouble distinguishing the risks in derivative trading as being any different from those of gambling and thus see no reason to help enforce obligations between derivatives traders. One way or the other, however, more countries than ever are being drawn into the orbit of the global derivatives market, in which there is no way to get "a little bit pregnant" because one derivative instrument naturally breeds an offspring. In this sense one derivative is all a government needs to permit for the entire chain, eventually unstable, of derivative promises to collapse, due to the linguistic fragility at the heart of the derivative form.

Thus the global ambitions of finance as a discipline match those of the derivative as a form. In both regards, the self-emancipation of the discipline of finance from its parent field of economics is the most momentous development of our times. For it allows financialized forms, such as the derivative, to become both *universal* and *global*: their universality has to do with their reliance, almost entirely on mathematical models of options pricing, of volatility, of portfolio risk, and of conceptual freedom from the world of the underlying asset. Neoclassical economics, let us recall, however mathematical its appearance, is resolutely about the prices and values of underlying commodities, and thus it is no surprise that the study of risk was virtually handed over by economics to business schools, as a matter for those concerned with the practical business of moving money around, rather than the sophisticated business of sturdy markets, competition, and prices in a world of limited goods and services. Because derivatives, as assets, have no limit set by the real or natural world, they are subject not to the laws of economics, such as they might be, but only to the laws of finance, of the science of how money begets money. The global ambitions of finance are directly connected to this new order of universality, for few countries can resist the call of a market and its principal form—the derivative—which promises the possibility of wealth that is hundreds of times the gross domestic product of any one country or of the entire global economy. This limitless, gravity-free image of wealth without labor or limit is the Midas model that few countries can resist. Thus the derivative form commands increasing global play and harbors infinite global risk.

One way to contain this risk and to appropriate the wealth promised by derivatives in a nonpredatory manner is to imagine and mobilize a nonpredatory derivative logic, which could open a progressive politics of dividualism. This is the concluding argument of chapter 7. How can we build a politics of progressive dividualism against the logic of the broken promise, which is the inner logic of the regnant derivative form (as I argued in chapter 1)?

The Promise of Progressive Dividualism

I began this book by arguing that the derivative contract is an extreme form of contractualism. Its extremism lies in the fact that the promise between two individuals who make a derivatives contract is based on their divergent views of the probability of a future "credit event." What is flawed about this promise is not the performative logic in any given derivatives contract but the leveraging of promises across a large and indefinitely expansive derivative chain, in which the risks of any given promise cumulate into a fissive chain whose distance from the values of underlying commodities must eventually become insupportable, thus creating a mountain of promissory risk that is doomed to collapse, as it did in the subprime mortgage crisis of 2007–8.

I have also shown that the mortgage crisis opens to our view a pattern of predatory dividualism, in which the slicing and dicing of individuals into a variety of risk-bearing scores is then bundled up (securitized) to make the bundled dividuals the bearers of an increasingly abstract and systemic risk in which their capacity to unite as individuals is irretrievably eroded. Furthermore, all current forms of resistance, through unions, class actions, debt refusal movements, regulatory actions, shareholder protests, court cases against insider trading, and other forms of redress against the predatory dividualization of the regnant derivatives market are doomed to fail because their architecture poses the moral force of the individual against a process of dividualization that they neither understand nor endorse.

Against this logic, the only fruitful alternative can come from efforts to harness our progressive potential as *dividuals* against the predatory dividualization of the financial markets. This is, in the first instance, a politics of consciousness, in which we must begin by exploring the global archive of dividualist cosmologies. This archive has recently been the subject of renewed attention from anthropologists, as I have noted in chapter 7. It builds on the fact that the line between humans and the rest of nature has long been organized as a shifting, relational and vital economy in which the dilemmas of humans are invariably placed in wider cosmologies of energies, agencies, and materialities. This vitalist archive is also congruent with the emergent feminist arguments among some of the new materialists that have emerged in science and technology studies, such as Karen Barad (2007), Diana Coole and Samantha Frost (2010), and Stacy Alaimo (2010), who in various ways espouse a form of feminist posthumanism that reframes the problem of agency in ways that embrace views of vitality, energy, and environmentalism that link them to political theorists such as Jane Bennett (2010) and William Connolly (2013), who have roots in Spinoza and Bergson, key philosophers of the metaphysics of matter.

This dialogue about the forms of agency that place humans in a shifting relationship to the nonhuman world is not yet as richly connected across disciplines and epistemologies as it could be. The anthropologists concerned with relational ontologies, the feminists concerned with posthuman agency, the Deleuzians concerned with the shifting material assemblages, the Latourians driven by actor network ideas of format, code, and node, remain in relatively distinct scholarly niches. Yet their work pushes in overlapping directions that have direct relevance to my argument and my vision of what is possible in the realm of financial markets.

In the conclusion to chapter 7, I indicated that in order to generate a progressive dividualist politics, we would have to be prepared to rethink such elementary social categories as group, class, public, and community, in order to get out of that architecture of the social that assumes canonical individual of Western modernity as the elementary unit of the social. This is in the first place a challenge to a very basic part of our current common sense.

If we can begin to think of ourselves as agents composed of dynamic potentials for interaction ("dividuals") who enter into temporary associations with many other kinds of energies and agencies in the world, only some of which take the forms of what we now think of as the human individual, we open up a wealth of new possibilities for how we might consociate, assemble, organize, and energize our environments, parts of which are machinic, organic, and technical. Nor does this new sort of agency—the relational agency of dividuals—need to be devoid of politics, ethics, or language. But the forms of this new ethics and politics will not rest any more on a special, autonomous, or permanent domain for humans, in the manner that most Western forms of reason have taught us to expect and assume.

The classical modern Western contract rests on the foundation of the bounded, sovereign, normative, and interest-seeking individual. At its heart is the logic of the promise, a commitment by one such individual to another whose force lies in the reciprocal morality of individuals, thus conceived, to one another. The logic of the derivative—as a form of promise that rests on the likelihood of the failure of the promises of other such pairs of individuals—produces dis-individuated human parts through a predatory process that generates one promise from another, steadily eroding reciprocity, multiplying risk, and eventually producing systemic collapse.

The cure for this systemic weakness is not the repair of the force of promises but the repair and reconstruction of the idea of the individual to enable new sorts of solidarity between dividuals, agents whose very partiality may allow for new aggregations of aspiration, interest, and affiliation. This amounts to no less than a new ideology of sociality. Fortunately we do not lack examples of such possibilities in the archives of human experience. Of course, it is no easy thing to bring into the ethics and politics of the modern world a form of agentive humanity that has been forgotten and marginalized in the process that rendered our modern view of the individual both natural and indispensable. It is a deeply political task, one that will require critique, argument, suasion, and mobilization. Its appeal is the promise of the massive wealth that the derivative form can deliver without the equally massive and unfair breaking of promises by a few individuals to many.

CHAPTER NINE

THE END OF THE CONTRACTUAL PROMISE

I began this book with the claim that the financial failure of 2007–8 was principally a failure of language. More exactly, I argued that the failure was of the linguistic form we normally call a promise, which I treat as an Austinian performative, an illocutionary speech act that creates the reality it refers to by its very utterance. I subsequently showed that if we look closely at the idea of the performative, we can see that what failed in the financial markets in 2007–8 was not any single promise (reflected in a particular derivatives trade) but the chain of promises created in the derivatives market that increases the distance between any given promise and the subsequent promise made with reference to it as an underlying asset. Through this chain, the derivatives market makes it possible to make contractual wagers based on prior promises, generating profit through differential assessments of the future risk of an upward or a downward movement in the price of the monetized contract which the derivative further monetizes. In effect, the derivative is a market in promises, each of which leverages a prior promise.

I also argued that our understanding of the world of derivative trading has much to gain from considering the anthropological tradition that looks at all rituals from a performative point of view, as actions that produce their effects by the effectiveness of their enacted forms. I further showed that derivatives appear to work through a certain form of retro-performativity in which they produce their own conditions of possibility by acting as if they already existed before the trade that produced them. In making this case, I was careful to point out that the analogy between derivative traders and primitives, between the trading floor and the corroboree, between gifts and derivative markets, should not be carried too far.

The principal reason for my qualification can now be directly engaged. Though Mauss's classic essay on *The Gift* (1990) was his effort to explain the underlying moral force of the modern contract, he was conscious that he had provided a pedigree and not a full account of the modern contract. The problem of the force and destiny of the modern legal contract remains elusive.

Today, contract lawyers and theorists actively debate the links between the modern contract and the promise as a linguistic act. The modern idea of contract is a foundational element of modern social thought. Without this idea, much of modern law, morality, and economy would fall apart. The debate about the nature of the contract goes back to Hobbes, who famously saw the way out of the state of nature as the emergence of the sovereign, who, among other things, is the final reason why individuals keep their promises to one another. Since Hobbes, there has been a rich debate about the ethics, the legal implications, and the force behind the promise. These debates turn crucially on how promises are to be understood, and contract theorists have debated whether their force lies in the nature of rules, conventions, and agreements (a position sometimes described as deontological) or whether it lies in some form of rational utilitarianism, whether of intentions or of consequences. [1]

Not all of this debate concerns me, spanning as it does some difficult issues in ethics, law, and political theory. My own position allies itself with the major book by Charles Fried (1981), which continues to be debated and contains a strong defense of the view of contracts as essentially promises. In Fried's view, their force can only be understood on the basis of the modern agreement to abide by a set of rules or conventions that precede rational calculations of self-interest, rather than on the basis of fear of the coercive force of the sovereign or of the potential beneficial consequences that follow from a general social agreement to abide by promises. Fried builds on a broader tradition of work on promises that includes John Searle, John Rawls, and others who were influenced both by Wittgenstein's view of ordinary language and by J. L. Austin's later development of Wittgenstein's views.

The general consensus that emerges from this view of the relationship of promise to contract, in spite of differences between the scholars who belong to it, is that while contracts may have other secondary features that give them their wide and deep role in modern legal and moral life, the foundation of this force lies in the promissory logic of the contract. The essence of Fried's position is that any variety of utilitarian, interest-centered view of the promise, and thus of the contract, is bound to run into difficulties. He therefore argues forcefully for a view of the promise as founded on a Kantian type of imperative that combines the placing of trust by one free individual in another with the entailment of a duty to fulfill—act upon—that promise in the future. In short, this argument, different forms of which are to be found in different authors who work in this tradition, shows the foundational, necessary, and powerful links between the free individual of the modern dispensation, what the promise says and the action it presages, and the dependence of *all* modern contracts on this principle.

Now I return to my view of the financial collapse of 2007–8 as a linguistic failure and, more exactly, as the failure of a fissive chain of promises, each of which is a contract that meets Fried's conditions of duty, freedom, and trust. Why does the system come to the edge of collapse? I have argued that the collapse has to do with the way in which promises in the derivatives market are based on leveraging previous promises, which have already been subject to de-individuation (the slicing and dicing of persons). The leveraging dimension is vital because the packaging together of promises into bundles that can be revalued and resold progressively frees any derivative to add value to the previous components of the promissory bundle as it also adds risk to the promissory chain. This freedom to add value is possible because of the new and increasingly risky wagers about future value (price) that can serially be made. What is new about this promissory logic is the capacity of any derivative to monetize previous promises, without regard to the disposition of the prior promises that are its basis or the future promises that may lie further down the promissory chain. This is the general danger that derivatives create in the chain of contracts that they indefinitely leverage and extend.

In addition, the idea of the *swap* (as in the credit default swap discussed in the previous chapter) is a particularly corrosive new addition to the existing family of derivatives, which also includes options and futures. The swap is a form of hedging by betting that party A (in a deal between A and B) will default on A's side of the deal, thus allowing party C and party D to make a mutually binding promise (contract) about the likelihood of such a default. Given that parties C and D have no direct interest or investment in the assets involved in the deal between A and B, the credit default swap between C and D is purely *speculative*. Looked at from the point of view that sees derivative contracts as a type of promise (performative in form), the credit default swap is actually a speculative bet on the certainty that one of the two parties who made a promise will *break* the promise.

It is hard to overstate the momentousness of this innovation, for it not only leverages one promise on another, as all derivative contracts do, but it actually makes it possible for one group of promisors to make money when a part of another pair's promise is broken. Such bundles of promises in the CDS market at the end of the first half of 2008 were worth $55 trillion (Sirri 2008), which amounted to almost 10 percent of the overall derivatives market. In short, in the middle of 2008, there was a sum of $55 trillion at play in the market for broken promises.

Since 2008, the CDS form has come in for considerable blame as the root of the financial disaster, and central bankers throughout the world are looking for ways in which to control its excesses, to limit its speculative potential, and to tighten the regulatory net around it. Partly in response to this scrutiny the US market and the worldwide market in CDS, where it existed, has seen significant declines since 2008. But the CDS horse is now out of the barn and, though it can be regulated in a number of ways, there is a deep contradiction in the approach of governments and traders to the potential of the swap—the bet on the certainty of broken promises. Where governments worry about run-away speculation leading to a general meltdown, as happened in the United States in 2007–8, traders in swaps see a market in the hundreds of trillions that should not go to waste.

For our purposes, the CDS is a symptom of a deeper and more tectonic process. Insofar as the CDS is a derivative contract and any derivative itself is an entirely legitimate contractual way to make money out of its underlying assets, the idea that there can be profit-making contracts that rest on the default of other contracts is a revolution in the history of capitalism, in which profit can now be made by the strategic identification of the likelihood of a failed promise. The current form of the CDS may well be managed, contained, and detoxified but it is virtually certain that new forms will emerge, one step ahead of the regulators, which exploit the principle of contracts that rely on the violation of other contracts.

To look at this development in the very heart of today's capitalism, we can benefit from Joseph Schumpeter's idea of "creative destruction" (1942), his heterodox homage to Marx, in which he argued that the most important innovations that capitalism both encouraged and guaranteed were those that entailed the destruction of those regimes of technology, labor, and solidarity on which its growth had previously depended. In other words, innovation in capitalism is its constitutive tendency, and is always only one step ahead of its own conditions of emergence, leaving massive destruction in its wake as it seeks new sources of profit through risk-taking.

The CDS form of the derivative is in this sense a radical Schumpeterian innovation. It uses the means of contract to erode the very basis of contracts since it involves promises that rest on failed promises. How long can the contract as a fundamental principle of modern Western society survive an entrepreneurial form of this type, which opens untold profit based on the growing potential for defaults in the highly financialized economy? Put another way, when risk on risk becomes the main source of profit, and when one of these risks is the upside risk of a reliable number of defaults (broken promises), can we not see here a Schumpeterian potential for the death of the contract as a foundational moral and social form?

If this scenario is even plausible, then we can ask two questions, one of which pertains to the contract as a modern form and the other to the idea of the individual that the modern contract both assumes and enhances. I have just indicated the potential self-destruction of the contractual form as it comes to cannibalize itself through the form of the credit default swap. I have also, especially in chapter 7, discussed the difference between the predatory dividualization produced by contemporary finance and an alternate form of dividualism that might allow us to open a different sort of politics for our deeply financialized times.

The proposal on which I would like to end this book builds on the argument about the dividual as a social form in chapters 7 and 8, and adds to it the possibility that the modern contract may not be able to withstand the monetized, dividualized, and leveraged pressure on the linguistic form of the promise itself. The normal solution to this sort of argument is to propose new sorts of regulation, which in turn rely on repairing the gaps, loopholes, and limits of the contract form. But what if we come to see that the contract as a social form is on the verge of "creative destruction" in Schumpeter's sense, as capital seeks its newest levels of risk-based profit through making promises against promises? In that case, the only resort may be to seek alliances, affiliations, linkages, and solidarities outside the individual as the human counterpart of the modern contract. Why not put our efforts into new forms of relationship, identification, agency, and solidarity that might be as dynamic, as inventive, and as shape-shifting as those of capital itself? These forms, as I have already argued, may be found in the archive of dividual ontologies that surround us in the anthropological record. This is not a plea for a return to the "before" or to the "other" of capitalism. It is a call to a different conception of the ground from which we can take risks, generate wealth, and pursue sociality on terms that, in leaving behind both the modern individual and the modern contract, have a reasonable chance of beating global finance at its own game. This is not an easy or an obvious political step, but creative destruction does not respect either normal science or politics as usual.

NOTES

Chapter One

1. Various scholars, including Michel Foucault (1966), Marc Shell (1982), Deirdre McCloskey (1985), William Maurer (2005), and Mary Poovey (2008) have studied the links between language and the economy, though with interests different from my own. Closer to my interest, and with a direct interest in performatives as a linguistic form relevant to contemporary finance, Benjamin Lee and Edward LiPuma have been working on the link between performatives, ritual, and the derivative form since 2004, and have helped me to clarify my own approach. Most recently, in a fascinating study of the speech practices of central bankers in the United States and Europe, Douglas Holmes (2013) has drawn on J. L. Austin in a manner highly compatible with my own, though he does not address the derivative as the quintessential instrument of contemporary finance or the modern contract as its underling social and moral form.

2. The question of how Marx, and subsequent Marxist scholars have engaged derivative finance is not without controversy. Marx himself was famously alert to the centrality of money to industrial capitalism and understood that labor value, and absolute and relative surplus value, both key concepts for him, were both measured and realized in the money form. What is also known is that Marx did understand the role of money in precapitalist economic formations, notably in the role of commercial interests in agriculture before the advent of industrialization. Marx certainly is the major modern thinker to have identified the specific ways in which money becomes the key to industrial capitalism, through the logic of the M-C-M formula, in the context of the labor theory of value. What is less clear is the extent to which Marx understood the potential of finance to become itself the key driver of capitalism, in the form of finance capitalism, an extension of his thought that had to wait for Rudolf Hilferding (1981). It is still another step, well after Hilferding, to get to the process of securitization (the systematic bundling of assets into tradable bonds), and the traffic in derivatives, a further step in the profitable trading of securities, on the basis of their capacity to contain unknown future values in current market prices. In short, Marx did not, and could not have, anticipated the market in risk itself that derivatives exploit and expand. Today, there is an active debate among Marxist scholars about how to bring a Marxist perspective to the process of massive wealth creation through the derivative form. Perhaps the best developed analysis of this type is to be

found in Bryan and Rafferty (2006), as well as in Martin (2002, 2007, 2015) and Grossberg (2010). These are brilliant efforts to construct a Marxist view of the derivative form, but they do not have a primary interest in the problem of promises, contracts, and performativity, as I do. Bryan and Rafferty's argument about "binding and blending" in the work of derivatives is especially resonant with my own line of argument. In my own group of close colleagues, in the Cultures of Finance group at New York University, Randy Martin, Robert Meister and Benjamin Lee have developed an interconnected view of volatility, optionality, and liquidity, linking Marx, Weber, and the logic of the derivative, which complements my own argument and promises a new basis for reading Marx in the light of derivative finance. I am grateful for Keith Hart's insistence that I make my understanding of Marxist approaches to finance more explicit.

3. The fuller discussion of the idea of the performative chain can be found in Appadurai 2015.

4. The modern American economy is built on the structure of contracts (for property, for jobs, for loans, for insurance, and for much else). But it is only the derivative contract that is part of a performative chain which is built on connections on a linked chain of securitized instruments, each of which lays the foundations for the next one, thus creating invisible bonds that reveal themselves mainly when liquidity disappears, buyers vanish and the markets collapse, or go into a temporary coma.

Chapter Two

1. The studies by Maurer, Miyazaki, and Riles are the most important accounts of the global flow of financial instruments and ideologies and thus are important sources for my own thought. Maurer's book (2005) is the first by an anthropologist to explore the cultural presuppositions of contemporary global finance. It is a close examination of the way in which the very object that comes to be Islamic banking is constituted by a global entanglement of conventional Western categories and efforts to render them legible, productive, and legitimate in various Islamic economies. Maurer's single most important accomplishment is to unsettle the idea of the difference between standard and "different" forms of financial practice and to insist that Islamic banking is as much a part of any contemporary financial order as its Western counterparts. This claim is both consistent with and further built upon by Annelise Riles (2011), in her study of the global circulation of the idea and practice of "collateral," which has several remarkable features, including its close study of a circulating legal form, its emphasis on the way in which an apparently recessive feature of Western contracts forces to be the pivot of both financial innovation and cultural translation, and of the ways in which law is the critical infrastructure of contemporary financial models and instruments. I

regard the pioneer works of Maurer and Riles as reflecting, along with the work of Douglas Holmes (2013), a new paradigm for linking legal, linguistic, and sociocultural logics in the world of derivative finance, to which I hope this book is also a contribution. An exceptional study of the way in which contemporary financial logics enter the life worlds of non-Western societies is Hiro Miyazaki's book (2013) on the ethos and ethics of arbitrage among a group of credit traders in Tokyo. An exercise in what the author calls the "ethnography of thinking," Miyazaki's study sets the standard for examining how a highly specific feature of contemporary financial markets—arbitrage—enters the life worlds of Japanese traders and shapes a sense of uncertainty, ambiguity, and transience that goes far beyond their technical practices. It also opens the space for a deep reversal of Weber's argument about the spirit of capitalism, since it sees the ethos of arbitrage as moving from technical spaces outward to everyday life, rather than as a force that comes from a broader cultural framework to animate economic practice. These and other implications of Miyazaki's work will doubtless engage many scholars in this field in the coming years.

2. Frank Knight's classic work on risk and uncertainty is still being debated and refined by economists and statisticians. In essence, Knightian uncertainty (as opposed to risk in Knight's definition) has to do with randomness in future events, which cannot be modeled probabilistically. It is thus about uncertainty outside the parameters of number, of probability, or of any form of statistical reason. What is Knightian about it is that it affects all probabilistic models of risk but cannot be technically encompassed by them. One example of a non-Knightian uncertainty would be a question such as: "Will God save the world?" that is certainly a matter of uncertainty but is not relevant to modeling risk in the economy.

Chapter Three

1. Michel Callon's view of performativity is largely focused on the discipline of economics, and consists of the observation that contemporary markets, including financial ones, are produced by economics, which defines both objects and agency in a manner that produces the effect of creating practices that enact, and thus confirm, the assumptions of the disciplinary model. He and his followers have no special interest in the derivative form as a special instance of Austinian performativity, the latter being vital to my own argument, which leads from the Austin's view of performatives, and thus to promises and to contracts.

2. *Wikipedia*, s.v. "Frank Knight," http://en.wikipedia.org/w/index.php?title=Frank_Knight&oldid=631969341.

3. An interesting exception is the 2006 paper by D. Beunza and R. Garud on "Frame-Making: An Interpretive Approach to Valuation under Knightian Uncertainty." In this paper the authors seek to make a strong argument about the importance

of calculative "frame-making" as the key to analysts' valuations of companies in conditions of Knightian uncertainty. They are critical of Bayesian approaches (which dominate the financial literature) and the "imitation" approach, which dominates behavioral economics. The frame-making approach of Beunza and Garud, derived from Erving Goffman's analysis of "frames" (1974), is reasonable and adequate for analyzing the rhetoric, diversity, and differential uptake of analysts' reports, but it leaves open the question of what more general intuitions about the economy determine large-scale decisions by major institutional players, such as short sellers and hedge-fund managers, who are more direct reflections of decisions in the face of Knightian uncertainty. This latter group is of primary relevance to my argument in this chapter. A recent set of arguments about the limitations of an excessive focus on risk, at the expense of uncertainty converges with my own views and is to be found in Rabinow and Samimian-Darash (2015).

4. Such contrarians do of course assume a wider world of traders who read risk more conventionally, and insofar as they are betting against them, they too depend on the models and measures of risk that saturate the financial markets. But they are also willing to use some sort of contrarian intuition (their channeling of Knightian uncertainty) to play uncertainty off against risk.

Chapter Four

1. The Black-Scholes model was produced in 1973 and remains both the Bible and the black box for options pricing by derivatives traders. Its history has been closely studied by MacKenzie (2009) and its strange status as a model in spite of many flaws that have been found in it since 1973 is discussed by Derman (2011). The essence of the Black-Scholes model is that it allows traders to price options. The model was based on a partial differential equation, now called the *Black–Scholes equation*, which estimates the price of the option over time. The key idea behind the model is to hedge the option by buying and selling the underlying asset in just the right way and, as a consequence, to eliminate risk. This type of hedging is called delta hedging and is the basis of more complicated hedging strategies such as those engaged in by investment banks and hedge funds. It could be argued that the Black-Scholes model and formula is the single most important mathematical tool which permitted the radical expansion of the derivatives market in the last four decades.

Chapter Seven

1. This chapter owes a special debt to all the members of the Cultures of Finance group at the Institute for Public Knowledge at New York University: Benjamin Lee, Edward LiPuma, Randy Martin, Robert Meister, and Robert Wosnitzer.

They prodded me to flesh out my ideas about the "dividual," and our conversations over the last three years have contributed immeasurably to this chapter.

2. For an excellent overview of this burgeoning field, see Diana Coole and Samantha Frost (2010).

3. My understanding of the story of the subprime mortgage crisis of 2007–8 is deeply indebted to Michael Lewis's riveting book, *The Big Short* (2010).

4. For a superb synoptic account of the political and ethical implications of the explosion in "big data," see Alice Marwick (2014).

5. See Alan Schrift (1997) for a superb overview of this French genealogy.

6. My understanding of performatives, as well as of retro-performativity, owes a great deal to many years of conversations with Benjamin Lee, who shares my University of Chicago graduate school immersion in cultural anthropology, and brings to the table a strong grasp of financial formalizations as well as linguistic forms and practices.

7. The idea of the dividual is having a welcome revival in contemporary anthropology due to a series of arguments about comparative cosmology by such thinkers as Viveiros de Castro (2012), Descola (2013), and Sahlins (2013). This development promises a dialogue with new trends in science and technology studies and the new materialisms, as I propose in chapter 8.

8. Elie Ayache's *The Blank Swan* (2010) is the first serious work of social science and philosophy to examine the critical role of backward equations, backward causalities, and backward narratives as critical features of the logic of derivative trading.

9. Here my argument is especially indebted to my colleagues in the Cultures of Finance group at New York University, who have alerted me to the complexities of liquidity, surplus value, volatility, and spreads in the categories and practices of contemporary finance, and the ways in which these forms can be mined for their immanent and socially generated wealth.

Chapter Eight

1. David Graeber takes up the subject of debt in his recent book on *Debt: The First 5000 Years* (2011), which is, among other things, a veritable manifesto for the debt-refusal movement in general and for the Occupy movement in Wall Street and beyond in 2014. This is not the place for a full engagement with this book, especially since it does not pay much attention on the last thirty years of the last 5,000, and thus has little to say about derivatives in particular or about the current financial markets generally, except to dismiss them as the nadir of the evil history of debt and its beneficiaries, such as bankers, moneylenders, and loan sharks from the beginnings of time. Graeber sees no hope whatsoever for redemption in the new financial instruments, and thus does not add much to what any close reader of Marx and Weber could have said about our current circumstances.

2. "Statistics: Statistics and Data Pertaining to Financial Markets and the Economy," *SIFMA*, http://www.sifma.org/research/statistics.aspx (accessed January 2, 2015).

3. "Objectives of the Reserve Bank of India," n.d., Reserve Bank of India. http://rbi.org.in/scripts/CommunicationPolicy.aspx (accessed January 2, 2015).

Chapter Nine

1. For an excellent overview of these debates, see Allen Habib (2009).

REFERENCES

Alaimo, Stacy. 2010. *Bodily Natures: Science, Environment, and the Material Self.* Bloomington, IN: Indiana University Press.

Appadurai, Arjun, ed. 1986. *The Social Life of Things: Commodities in Cultural Perspective.* Cambridge: Cambridge University Press.

———. 2001. "Deep Democracy: Urban Governmentality and the Horizon of Politics." *Environment and Urbanization* 13 (2): 23–43. doi:10.1177/095624780101300203.

———. 2004. *The Capacity to Aspire: Culture and the Terms of Recognition.* In *Culture and Public Action*, edited by Vijayendra Rao and Michael Walton, 59–84. Stanford, CA: Stanford University Press.

———. 2012. "The Spirit of Calculation." *Cambridge Anthropology* 30 (1): 3–17. doi:10.3167/ca.2012.300102.

———. 2013. *The Future as Cultural Fact: Essays on the Global Condition.* London: Verso.

———. 2015. "Success and Failure in the Deliberative Economy." In *Reclaiming Democracy: Judgment, Responsibility and the Right to Politics*, edited by Albena Azmanova and Mihaela Mihai. New York: Routledge.

Austin, J. L. 1962. *How to Do Things with Words: The William James Lectures Delivered at Harvard University in 1955*, edited by J. O. Urmson and Marina Sbisa. Oxford: Clarendon Press.

Ayache, Elie. 2010. *The Blank Swan: The End of Probability.* Chichester, West Sussex: Wiley.

Baldwin, James. 1963. *The Fire Next Time.* New York: Vintage International.

Barad, Karen. 2007. *Meeting the Universe Halfway: Quantum Physics and the Entanglement of Matter and Meaning.* Durham, NC: Duke University Press.

Beck, Ulrich. 1992. *Risk Society: Towards a New Modernity.* Newbury Park, CA: SAGE Publications.

Bennett, Jane. 2010. *Vibrant Matter: A Political Ecology of Things.* Durham, NC: Duke University Press.

Beunza, D., and R. Garud. 2006. "Frame-making: An Interpretive Approach to Valuation under Knightian Uncertainty." Working Paper. New York: Columbia University.

Beunza, Daniel, and David Stark. 2004. "Tools of the Trade: The Socio-Technology of Arbitrage in a Wall Street Trading Room." *Industrial and Corporate Change* 13 (2): 369–400. doi:10.1093/icc/dth015.

Boas, Franz. 1921. *Ethnology of the Kwakiutl (Based on Data Collected by George Hunt)*. Thirty-Fifth Annual Report of the Bureau of American Ethnology, 1913–1914. Washington, DC: Government Printing Office.

Bourdieu, Pierre. 1976. *Outline of a Theory of Practice*. Translated by Richard Nice. Cambridge: Cambridge University Press.

Brentano, L. 2011. *Ethics and Economics in History*. Paderborn: Salzwasser-Verlag GmbH. Originally published in 1901.

Brouwer, Maria T. 2003. "Weber, Schumpeter and Knight on Entrepreneurship and Economic Development." In *Change, Transformation and Development*, edited by John Stan Metcalfe and Uwe Cantner, 145–67. Heidelberg: Physica-Verlag. http://dx.doi.org/10.1007/978-3-7908-2720-0_9.

Brown, Michael F. 1997. *The Channeling Zone: American Spirituality in an Anxious Age*. Cambridge, MA: Harvard University Press.

Bryan, Dick, and Michael Rafferty. 2006. *Capitalism with Derivatives: A Political Economy of Financial Derivatives, Capital, and Class*. New York: Palgrave Macmillan.

Butler, Judith. 1990. *Gender Trouble: Feminism and the Subversion of Identity*. New York: Routledge.

———. 1997. *Excitable Speech: A Politics of the Performative*. New York: Routledge.

———. 2004. *Undoing Gender*. New York: Routledge.

Callon, M. 1998. *Laws of the Markets*. Malden, MA: Blackwell.

Callon, Michel, Yuval Millo, and Fabian Muniesa, eds. 2007. *Market Devices*. Malden, MA: Blackwell.

Cetina, Karin Knorr, and Alex Preda. 2007. "The Temporalization of Financial Markets: From Network to Flow." *Theory, Culture, and Society* 24 (7–8): 116–38. doi: 10.1177/0263276407084700.

Cohan, William D. 2009. *House of Cards: A Tale of Hubris and Wretched Excess on Wall Street*. New York: Doubleday.

Comaroff, Jean, and John L. Comaroff. 2000. "Millennial Capitalism: First Thoughts on a Second Coming." *Public Culture* 12 (2): 291–343. doi:10.1215/08992363-12-2-291.

Connolly, William E. 2013. *The Fragility of Things: Self-Organizing Processes, Neoliberal Fantasies, and Democratic Activism*. Durham, NC: Duke University Press.

Coole, Diana, and Samantha Frost, eds. 2010. *New Materialisms: Ontology, Agency, and Politics*. Durham, NC: Duke University Press.

Davidson, Paul. 1994. *Post Keynesian Macroeconomic Theory: A Foundation for Successful Economic Policies for the Twenty-First Century*. Aldershot: Edward Elgar.

Debord, Guy. 2007. "Theory of the Dérive." *Les Lèvres Nues* #9. Translated by Ken Knabb. Berkeley, CA: Bureau of Public Secrets. Originally published in 1956.

Deleuze, Gilles. 1992. "Postscript on the Societies of Control." *October* 59:3–7. doi: 10.2307/778828.

Deleuze, Gilles, and Félix Guattari. 1987. *A Thousand Plateaus: Capitalism and Schizophrenia*. Translated by Brian Massumi. Minneapolis: University of Minnesota Press.

Derman, Emanuel. 2011. *Models. Behaving. Badly: Why Confusing Illusion with Reality Can Lead to Disaster, on Wall Street and in Life*. New York: Free Press.

Derrida, Jacques. 1992. *Given Time: I. Counterfeit Money*. Translated by Peggy Kamuf. Chicago: University of Chicago Press.

Descola, Philippe. 2013. *Beyond Nature and Culture*. Translated by Janet Lloyd. Chicago: University of Chicago Press.

Dumont, Louis. 1970. *Homo Hierarchicus: The Caste System and Its Implications*. Chicago: University of Chicago Press.

Durkheim, Emile. 1995. *The Elementary Forms of Religious Life*. Translated by Karen E. Fields. New York: Free Press. Originally published in 1912.

Evans-Pritchard, E. 1940. *The Nuer: A Description of the Modes of Livelihood and Political Institutions of a Nilotic People*. Oxford: Clarendon Press.

Fortes, Meyer. 1973. "On the Concept of the Person among the Tallensi." In *La notion de personne en Afrique noire*, edited by R. Bastide and G. Dieterle, 238–319. Acte du Colloque international du CNRS 544. Paris: Colloques Internationaux du Centre National de la Recherche Scientifique.

Foucault, Michel. 1966. *The Order of Things*. Paris: Editions Gallimard.

Fried, Charles. 1981. *Contract as Promise*. Cambridge, MA: Harvard University Press.

Geertz, Clifford. 1972. "Deep Play: Notes on the Balinese Cockfight." *Daedalus* 101 (1): 1–37. doi:10.2307/20024056.

———. 1978. "The Bazaar Economy: Information and Search in Peasant Marketing." *American Economic Review* 68 (2): 28–32. doi:10.2307/1816656.

Geschiere, Peter. 1997. *The Modernity of Witchcraft: Politics and the Occult in Postcolonial Africa*. Charlottesville: University of Virginia Press.

Ginsburg, Faye D., and Rayna Rapp, eds. 1995. *Conceiving the New World Order: The Global Politics of Reproduction*. Berkeley: University of California Press.

Girard, René. 1977. *Violence and the Sacred*. Translated by Patrick Gregory. Baltimore, MD: Johns Hopkins University Press.

Goffman, Erving. 1974. *Frame Analysis: An Essay on the Organization of Experience*. Cambridge, MA: Harvard University Press.

Gordon, Colin, ed. 1980. "Afterword." In *Power/Knowledge: Selected Interviews and Other Writings, 1972–1977* by Michel Foucault, 229–60. New York: Vintage.

Graeber, David. 2011. *Debt: The First 5,000 Years*. Brooklyn, NY: Melville House.

Grossberg, Lawrence. 2010. "Modernity and Commensuration." *Cultural Studies* 24 (3): 295–332. doi:10.1080/09502381003750278.

Grossein, Jean-Pierre, ed. and trans. 1996. "Introduction." In *The Sociology of Religion* by Max Weber. Paris: Gallimard.

Guyer, Jane I. 2007. "Prophecy and the Near Future: Thoughts on Macroeconomic, Evangelical, and Punctuated Time." *American Ethnologist* 34 (3): 409–21. doi:10.1525/ae.2007.34.3.409.

Habib, Allen. 2009. "Promises to the Self." *Canadian Journal of Philosophy* 39 (4): 537–57.

Hacking, Ian. 1992. "The Self-Vindication of the Laboratory Sciences." In *Science as Practice and Culture*, edited by Andrew Pickering, 29–64. Chicago: University of Chicago Press.

Hart, Keith. 2000. *The Memory Bank: Money in an Unequal World.* London: Profile Books.

Heelas, Paul. 2008. *Spiritualities of Life: New Age Romanticism and Consumptive Capitalism.* Malden, MA: Wiley-Blackwell.

Hilferding, Rudolf. 1981. *Finance Capital. A Study of the Latest Phase of Capitalist Development.* Translated by Morris Watnick and Sam Gordon. Edited by Tom Bottomore. London: Routledge and Kegan Paul. Originally published in 1910.

Hirschman, Albert O. 1977. *The Passions and the Interests: Political Arguments for Capitalism before its Triumph.* Princeton, NJ: Princeton University Press.

Holmes, Douglas R. 2013. *Economy of Words: Communicative Imperatives in Central Banks.* Chicago: University of Chicago Press.

Janeway, William H. 2006. "Risk versus Uncertainty: Frank Knight's 'Brute' Facts of Economic Life." Last modified June 7, 2006. http://privatizationofrisk.ssrc.org/Janeway/.

Kahneman, Daniel, and Amos Tversky. 1979. "Prospect Theory: An Analysis of Decision under Risk." *Econometrica* 47 (2): 263–91. doi:10.2307/1914185.

Knight, Frank H. 2009. *Risk, Uncertainty, and Profit.* Kissimmee, FL: Signalman. Originally published in 1921.

Latour, Bruno. 2005. *Reassembling the Social: An Introduction to Actor-Network Theory.* Oxford: Oxford University Press.

Leach, Edmund. 1976. *Culture and Communication: The Logic by which Symbols Are Connected: An Introduction to the Use of Structuralist Analysis in Social Anthropology.* Cambridge: Cambridge University Press.

Lears, Jackson. 2003. *Something for Nothing: Luck in America.* New York: Viking.

Levi-Strauss, Claude. 1976. *Structural Anthropology*, vol. 2. Translated by Monique Layton. Chicago: University of Chicago Press.

Levitt, Steven D., and Stephen J. Dubner. 2005. *Freakonomics: A Rogue Economist Explores the Hidden Side of Everything.* New York: Harper Perennial.

Lewis, Michael. 2010. *The Big Short: Inside the Doomsday Machine.* New York: Norton.

LiPuma, Edward, and Benjamin Lee. 2004. *Financial Derivatives and the Globalization of Risk.* Durham, NC: Duke University Press.

MacKenzie, Donald. 2006. *An Engine, Not a Camera: How Financial Models Shape Markets.* Cambridge, MA: MIT Press.

———. 2009. *Material Markets: How Economic Agents Are Constructed.* Oxford: Oxford University Press.

MacKenzie, Donald, Fabian Muniesa, and Lucia Siu, eds. 2007. *Do Economists Make Markets?: On the Performativity of Economics.* Princeton, NJ: Princeton University Press.

Malinowski, Bronislaw. 1922. *Argonauts of the Western Pacific.* New York: E. P. Dutton and Co.

Marriott, McKim. 1976. "Hindu Transactions: Diversity without Dualism." In *Transaction and Meanning: Directions in the Anthropology of Exchange and Symbolic Behavior,* edited by Bruce Kapferer, 109–42. Philadelphia, PA: Institute for the Study of Human Issues.

Marriott, McKim, and Ronald Inden. 1974. "Caste Systems." In *Encyclopaedia Britannica.* 15th ed., 3:982–91.

Martin, Randy. 2002. *Financialization of Daily Life.* Philadelphia, PA: Temple University Press.

———. 2007. *An Empire of Indifference: American War and the Financial Logic of Risk Management.* Durham, NC: Duke University Press.

———. 2011. *Under New Management: Universities, Administrative Labor, and the Professional Turn.* Philadelphia, PA: Temple University Press.

———. 2015. *Knowledge LTD: Toward a Social Logic of the Derivative.* Philadelphia, PA: Temple University Press.

Marwick, Alice E. 2014. "How Your Data Are Being Deeply Mined." *New York Review of Books,* January 9. http://www.nybooks.com/articles/archives/2014/jan/09/how-your-data-are-being-deeply-mined/.

Marx, Karl. 1992. *Capital.* Vol. 1, *A Critique of Political Economy.* Translated by Ben Fowkes. New York: Penguin Classics. Originally published in 1867.

Maurer, William. 2005. *Mutual Life, Limited: Islamic Banking, Alternative Currencies, Lateral Reason.* Princeton, NJ: Princeton University Press.

Mauss, Marcel. 1985. "A Category of the Human Mind: The Notion of Person; the Notion of Self." Translated by W. D. Halls. In *The Category of the Person: Anthropology, Philosophy, History,* edited by Michael Carrithers, Steven Collins, and Steven Lukes, 1–25. Cambridge: Cambridge University Press. Originally published in 1938.

———.1990. *The Gift: The Form and Reason for Exchange in Archaic Societies.* Translated by W. D. Halls. London: Routledge Classics. Originally published in *L'Année Sociologique* in 1925.

McCloskey, Deirdre N. 1985. *The Rhetoric of Economics.* Madison: University of Wisconsin Press.

Meyer, Birgit. 1999. *Translating the Devil: Religion and Modernity among the Ewe in Ghana*. Trenton, NJ: Africa World Press.

Miller, Peter. 2008. "Calculating Economic Life." *Journal of Cultural Economy* 1 (1): 51–64. doi:10.1080/17530350801913643.

Miller, Peter, Liisa Kurunmäki, and Ted O'Leary. 2008. "Accounting, Hybrids and the Management of Risk." *Accounting, Organizations and Society* 33 (7–8): 942–67. doi:10.1016/j.aos.2007.02.005.

Mitchell, Timothy. 1998. "Fixing the Economy." *Cultural Studies* 12 (1): 82–101. doi:10.1080/095023898335627.

Miyazaki, Hirokazu. 2007. "Between Arbitrage and Speculation: An Economy of Belief and Doubt." *Economy and Society* 36 (3): 396–415. doi:10.1080/03085140701428365.

———. 2013. *Arbitraging Japan: Dreams of Capitalism at the End of Finance*. Berkeley: University of California Press.

Morris, Charles R. 2008. *The Trillion Dollar Meltdown: Easy Money, High Rollers, and the Great Credit Crash*. New York: Public Affairs.

Myers, Fred R. 2002. *Painting Culture: The Making of an Aboriginal High Art*. Durham NC: Duke University Press.

Pálsson, Gísli, and Paul Rabinow. 1999. "Iceland: The Case of a National Human Genome Project." *Anthropology Today* 15 (5): 14. doi:10.2307/2678370.

Parfit, Derek. 1984. *Reasons and Persons*. Oxford: Oxford University Press.

Pollack, Sydney, dir. 1970. *They Shoot Horses, Don't They?* Film.

Poon, Martha A. 2008. "From New Deal Institutions to Capital Markets: Commercial Consumer Risk Scores and the Making of Subprime Mortgage Finance." *Accounting, Organizations and Society* 35 (5): 654–74.

Poovey, Mary. 2008. *Genres of the Credit Economy: Mediating Value in Eighteenth- and Nineteenth-Century Britain*. Chicago: University of Chicago Press.

Power, Michael. 1997. *The Audit Society: Rituals of Verification*. Oxford: Oxford University Press.

Rabinow, Paul, and Limor Samimian-Darash, eds. 2015. *Modes of Uncertainty: Anthropological Cases*. Chicago: University of Chicago Press.

Rao, Vijayendra, and Michael Walton. 2004. *Culture and Public Action*. Stanford, CA: Stanford Social Sciences.

Riles, Annelise. 2001. "Real Time: Governing the Market after the Failure of Knowledge." *Law and Economics Papers*, June. http://law.bepress.com/nwwps-lep/art41.

———. 2004. "Real Time: Unwinding Technocratic and Anthropological Knowledge." *American Ethnologist* 31 (3): 392–405. doi:10.1525/ae.2004.31.3.392.

———. 2011. *Collateral Knowledge: Legal Reasoning in the Global Financial Markets*. Chicago: University of Chicago Press.

Roitman, Janet. 2004. *Fiscal Disobedience: An Anthropology of Economic Regulation in Central Africa*. Princeton, NJ: Princeton University Press.

Rose, Nikolas. 1992. "Engineering the Human Soul: Analyzing Psychological Expertise." *Science in Context* 5 (2): 351- 69. doi:10.1017/S0269889700001228.

Rose, Nikolas, and Peter Miller. 2010. "Political Power beyond the State: Problematics of Government." *British Journal of Sociology* 61:271–303. doi:10.1111/j.1468-4446.2009.01247.

Sahlins, Marshall D. 1972. *Stone Age Economics*. Chicago: Aldine-Atherton.

———. 2013. *What Kinship Is—And Is Not*. Chicago: University of Chicago Press.

Sandel, Michael J. 2012. *What Money Can't Buy: The Moral Limits of Markets*. Thorndike, ME: Center Point.

Sassen, Saskia. 2006. *Territory, Authority, Rights: From Medieval to Global Assemblages*. Princeton, NJ: Princeton University Press.

Schelling, Thomas C. 1978. *Micromotives and Macrobehavior*. New York: W. W. Norton.

Schrift, Alan D. 1997. *The Logic of the Gift: Toward an Ethic of Generosity*. New York: Routledge.

Schumpeter, Joseph A. 2008. *Capitalism, Socialism, and Democracy*. New York: Harper Perennial. Originally published in 1942.

Shell, Marc. 1982. *Money, Language, and Thought: Literary and Philosophic Economies from the Medieval to the Modern Era*. Berkeley: University of California Press.

Simmel, Georg. 1978. *The Philosophy of Money*. Translated by Tom Bottomore and David Frisby. London: Routledge and Kegan Paul. Originally published in 1900.

Simon, Jeremy M. 2011. "Consumer Credit Card Debt Jumps Sharply." Last modified July 8, 2011. http://www.creditcards.com/credit-card-news/federal-reserve-g19-consumer-credit-may-2011-1276.php.

Sirri, Erik. 2008. "Testimony Concerning Credit Default Swaps." Last modified October 15, 2008. http://www.sec.gov/news/testimony/2008/ts101508ers.htm.

Sombart, Werner. 2001. *The Jews and Modern Capitalism*. Translated by M. Epstein. New York: E. P. Dutton. Originally published in 1911.

Strathern, Marilyn. 1988. *The Gender of the Gift: Problems with Women and Problems with Society in Melanesia*. Berkeley: University of California Press.

Tambiah, Stanley J. 1968. "The Magical Power of Words." *Man* 3 (2): 175. doi:10.2307/2798500.

———. 1985. "A Performative Approach to Ritual." In Tambiah, *Culture, Thought, and Social Action: An Anthropological Perspective*, 123–66. Cambridge, MA: Harvard University Press.

Tett, Gillian. 2009. *Fool's Gold: How the Bold Dream of a Small Tribe at J.P. Morgan Was Corrupted by Wall Street Greed and Unleashed a Catastrophe*. New York: Free Press.

Troeltsch, Ernst. 1992. *The Social Teaching of the Christian Churches.* Translated by Olive Wyon. Louisville, KY: Westminster/John Knox Press. Originally published in 1912.

Turner, Victor W. 1967. *The Forest of Symbols: Aspects of Ndembu Ritual.* Ithaca, NY: Cornell University Press.

van Gennep, Arnold. 1960. *The Rites of Passage.* Translated by Monika B. Vizedom and Gabrielle L. Caffee. Chicago: University of Chicago Press. Originally published in 1909.

Viveiros de Castro, Eduardo. 2012. "Cosmological Perspectivism in Amazonia and Elsewhere." In *Hau Masterclass Series,* vol. 1. http://www.haujournal.org/index.php/masterclass/issue/view/Masterclass Volume 1.

Weber, Max. 2008. *Roman Agrarian History: In Its Relation to Roman Public Law and Civil Law.* Translated by Richard I. Frank. Claremont, CA: Regina Books. Originally published in 1891.

——. 2009. *The Protestant Ethic and the Spirit of Capitalism.* Translated by Stephen Kalberg. Oxford: Oxford University Press. Originally published in 1905.

——. 1978. *Economy and Society: An Outline of Interpretive Sociology.* Edited by Guenther Roth and Claus Wittich. Translated by Ephraim Fischoff et al. Berkeley: University of California Press. Originally published in 1922.

——. 2003. *General Economic History.* Translated by Frank H. Knight. Mineola, NY: Dover. Originally published in 1923.

Weiner, Annette B. 1991. *Cloth and Human Experience.* Edited by Jane Schneider. Washington, DC: Smithsonian Books.

Wessel, David. 2010. *In FED We Trust: Ben Bernanke's War on the Great Panic.* New York: Crown Business.

Wosnitzer, Robert. 2014. "Desk, Firm, God, Country: Proprietary Trading and the Speculative Ethos of Financialism." PhD diss., New York University.

Yuran, Noam. 2014. *What Money Wants: An Economy of Desire.* Stanford, CA: Stanford University Press.

Zaloom, Caitlin. 2006. *Out of the Pits: Traders and Technology from Chicago to London.* Chicago: University of Chicago Press.

Zandi, Mark. 2008. *Financial Shock: A 360° Look at the Subprime Mortgage Implosion, and How to Avoid the Next Financial Crisis.* Harlow: FT Press.

INDEX